RABINDRANATH TAGORE

LETTERS TO A FRIEND

RABINDRANATH TAGORE

LETTERS TO A FRIEND

EDITOR

C. F. ANDREWS

GYAN

Published by

GYAN

Gyan Publishing House
5, Ansari Road
Daryaganj, New Delhi-110002
Phone: 011-47034999, 9811692060
E-mail: books@gyanbooks.com

Distribution Network
gyanbooks.com
India, USA, Canada, UK, Australia

ISBN: 978-93-7169-153-6 (PB)

First Published, 1928

2nd Impression 2025

Printed at: Gyan Press, Delhi.

RABINDRANATH TAGORE – LETTERS TO A FRIEND
Editor: C. F. ANDREWS

Rabindranath Tagore

From the dry point by Muirhead Bone

Rabindranath Tagore

LETTERS TO A FRIEND

Edited with

Two Introductory Essays by

C. F. ANDREWS

London

GEORGE ALLEN & UNWIN LTD

Museum Street

TO

THE MEMORY OF

W. WINSTANLEY PEARSON

PREFACE

THE letters contained in this volume were written to me by Rabindranath Tagore during the years 1913–1922. Many of them were published in India, in the *Modern Review*, and also in book form, under the title *Letters from Abroad*. The present volume represents an entire revision and enlargement of that book, of which only a few copies reached England. The material has now been divided into chapters, with a brief explanatory summary of the circumstances in which the letters were written.

It is a pleasure to me to thank Mr. Ramananda Chatterjee, editor of the *Modern Review*, and Mr. S. Ganesan, publisher, Madras, for permission to use the letters included in this volume, which have already appeared in India. I would also thank Messrs. Macmillan for leave to quote in full the poem on page 52, and Mr. Kelk for his kind help in proof correction.

With the Poet's sanction, this volume has been dedicated to the memory of my own dear friend and fellow-worker at Santiniketan, William Winstanley Pearson. He accompanied me on journeys undertaken with Rabindranath Tagore in different parts of the world, and also was my companion when I travelled with him alone to South Africa, Australia, New Zealand and Fiji. He was with the Poet in Europe and America at the time when many of these letters were written, and is often referred to in them. His death, owing to a railway accident in Italy in 1923—just when he was at the height of his powers of service and love—has made the fellowship between East and West, for which Santiniketan stands, doubly sacred to us all. He had two homes, one in Manchester and one at Santiniketan, both of them very dear to him. In each his memory is still fresh after the lapse of years.

Any profit from this book will be devoted to the Pearson Memorial Hospital at Santiniketan, which is open to our neighbours, the Santal aboriginals, as well as to the members of the Asram. Willie Pearson's great joy at Santiniketan was to visit these Santal villagers along with the boys of the Asram. He built a school and a well for them and did other acts of service. There could be no more suitable way of preserving his memory than such a hospital.

In conclusion, my special thanks are due to Muirhead Bone and Mukul Dey for their kindness in allowing me to use their drypoint etchings, and to William Rothenstein for the facsimile of the Poet's handwriting. They all shared with me the friendship of Willie Pearson, to whose memory this book is dedicated.

C. F. ANDREWS

October 1928

CONTENTS

ILLUSTRATIONS

AN ESSAY ON THE BENGAL RENAISSANCE

I

THE course taken by the Bengal Renaissance a hundred years ago was strangely similar to that of Western Europe in the sixteenth century. The result in the history of mankind is likely to be in certain respects the same also. For just as Europe awoke to new life then, so Asia is awakening to-day.

In Europe it was the shock of the Arab civilization and the Faith of Islam which startled the West out of the intellectual torpor of the Dark Ages. Then followed the recovery of the Greek and Latin Classics and a new interpretation of the Christian Scriptures, both of which, acting together, brought the full Reformation and Renaissance.

In Bengal it was the shock of the Western civilization that startled the East into new life and helped forward its wonderful rebirth. Then followed the revival of the Sanskrit Classics and a reformation from within of the old religions. These two forces, acting together, made the Bengal Renaissance a living power in Asia. In Bengal itself the literary and artistic movement came into greatest prominence. Rabindranath Tagore has been its crown.

II

Early in the nineteenth century the burning question in Bengal was whether the spread of the English language should be encouraged or not. Macaulay's famous minute, written in 1835, fixed the English tongue as the medium for higher education. "Never on earth," writes Sir John Seeley, "was a more momentous question discussed." The phrase is an arresting one, and appears a palpable exaggeration until we understand the issues involved, not only for Bengal, but for every country in the East.

Macaulay won the victory. Nevertheless, some of his premises were unsound and his conclusions inaccurate. He poured contempt on the Sanskrit Classics; he treated Bengali literature as useless. In expressing these opinions he committed egregious blunders. Yet, strangely enough, in spite of his narrow outlook, his practical insight was not immediately at fault. The hour for the indigenous revival had not yet come. A full shock from without was needed, and the study of English gave the shock required.

But the new life which first appeared was not altogether healthy. It led immediately to a shaking of old customs and an unsettlement of religious convictions, carried often to a violent and unthinking extreme. The greatest disturbance of all was in the social sphere. A wholesale imitation of purely Western habits led to a painful confusion of ideas. It was a brilliant and precocious age, bubbling over with a new vitality; but wayward and unregulated, like a rudderless ship on a stormy sea.

III

The one outstanding personality, whose presence saved Bengal at this crisis, was the great Raja Ram Mohun Roy. Towering above his contemporaries, solitary and majestic, this extraordinary genius seems to have measured accurately the force of every new current as it flowed quickly past, and to have steered his own course with an almost unerring precision. As practical as Macaulay, he was no mere opportunist. He was a true prophet, and had the prophet's sacred fire of enthusiasm. On the literary side he was one of the most ardent promoters of the new Western learning, and eagerly helped forward Macaulay's programme. But the best energies of his marvellously full life were directed to re-create in the heart of the Bengali people that true reverence for the Indian past which should lead to a revival of their own Sanskrit Classics. Above all, he did not despise his Bengali mother-tongue, but brought it back into full literary use.

IV

Debendranath Tagore, the father of Rabindranath, was the next outstanding figure in the Bengali literary revival. His work and influence lasted for more than half a century. If Ram Mohun Roy may be likened to the root of this tree of literature, planted deep in the soil, Debendranath Tagore may be compared to its strong and vigorous stem, and Rabindranath, his son, to its flower and fruit. Rarely in the history of literature can such a direct succession be traced.

Debendranath's religious character illuminated the age with a moral grandeur of its own. So impressive was his spiritual authority, that he received by universal consent the name of Maharshi, or great saint. During the flood-tide of English fashion he held fast to the ancient moorings and strengthened every bond which kept his country close to its own historic past.

His autobiography, translated by his son, reveals the deep religious spirit of modern Bengal, along with its passion for intellectual truth. The Tagore family had already been attracted within the orbit of Raja Ram Mohun Roy, and the vivid memory of the great reformer was one of the strongest influences in moulding the life of Debendranath as he grew up from boyhood to youth.

By the middle of the nineteenth century, owing to these initial movements, a creative period in

Bengali literary history had set in. It represented not merely an awakening of Bengal, but the beginning of a new era for the whole of Asia.

V

This Bengal Renaissance bears on its surface the marks of conflict between the new Western learning and the revived Sanskrit Classics. Toru Dutt, the fairest and frailest flower among the writers, composed her songs only in English; but the fragrance of the Sanskrit past pervades all her works and makes them a national possession. Michael Dutt began by writing English verse; but he abandoned this, while his literary powers were still at their height, and composed his later poems in a wonderfully sonorous and majestic Bengali metre. He has been called the Milton of the Bengal revival. Bankim's novels carry back the mind at every turn to the romance writers in the West. We can almost feel behind them the zest with which young Bengal explored their new-found treasures.

But the strength of the period consisted in this, that the writers, amid all their passionate and devoted study of English, remained true to the ancient Indian ideal. They remembered the rock from whence they were hewn. They did not despise their own birthright. Not only the language, but also the subjects, of this new literature were brought more in touch with the people. The village life of Bengal, which had tended to fall into the background, gained a new appreciation. The mediæval as well as the classical times were laid under contribution for subject-matter. The commanding ideal at last rose up before the minds of men, to build a truly national literature and art out of the living stones of indigenous poetry, music and song.

VI

Into this rich heritage of the past the young poet Rabindranath entered, and he has done more than anyone else to make this ideal a living inspiration in Bengal. A friend of mine has described to me the scene that took place when the aged novelist Bankim was being honoured and garlanded. The old man took the garland from off his own neck and placed it on that of a young writer who was seated at his feet—Rabindranath Tagore.

This act of Bankim has now been universally recognized as both generous and just. That which others were struggling to attain, in the midst of insuperable difficulties, Rabindranath has reached with the quick leap and joyful ease of supreme genius. The ideals of art, which were before only dimly discerned, he has seen with open vision. Moreover, in his later works he has carried still further the spiritual mission of his father, and he has clothed his own deepest religious thoughts with a raiment of simplicity and beauty.

His fame has come to the full in recent years, and his poetry has taken on a more prophetic tone. He has passed forward from the subjective period of unbounded delight in Nature, to enter into the mystery of the vast sorrow of the world; to share the heavy burden of the poor; to face death itself unmoved; to look for and attain the unclouded vision of God.

VII

In all this, Rabindranath has remained close to the heart of Bengal. Every day that I was with him, in 1912, his eyes seemed to be straining across the sea, to greet his boys at Santiniketan—longing also to be back among his village people at Shileida, among whom he was a father and a friend.

It is not wonderful, therefore, that Bengal, from whose soil he seems to draw his deepest inspiration, should have been inspired in turn by his music and song with a high consciousness of its own destiny. He has given vital expression, at a supreme moment of history, to the rising hopes of his own people. In that country of music and art and song,

> The prophetic soul of the wide world
> Dreaming of things to come

has found at last its vision in and through his poems. The dreams which Bengal is now dreaming may not all come true.

> The tumult and the shouting dies:
> The captains and the kings depart,

in the pageant of literature as well as that of empire. But song and music are mighty instruments, when the spirit of a rising people is beating high with hope; and to-day men, women, and even little children, are seeing through the eyes of Rabindranath the vision of "Golden Bengal."

That gracious vision is radiant and luminous. And there is not unmixed with it a sacred sense of awe, that God has visited His people.

If this supreme power of music and literature to create a new spirit in a whole people seems somewhat unreal in the West, it must be remembered that India still retains, deep below the surface, her living faith in the Unseen.

AN ESSAY ON THE PERSONALITY OF TAGORE

I

The temperament and character of Rabindranath Tagore may best be understood if I attempt to describe one memorable day in London, when he told me in outline the story of his own life in relation to his literary career.

He was lodging in the upper room of a house just outside the entrance to South Kensington Underground Station. The time was a morning in September 1912, and a thick London fog filled the air. He was still weak on account of a very serious illness, which had brought him to the West to undergo an operation, and his face looked pale and worn.

He first told me about his father—how all the household became still and hushed when he was present in the house, as if anxious not to disturb his meditations.

He spoke to me, also, about his mother, who had died when he was quite young. As he saw her face for the last time on earth, calm and beautiful in death, it awakened in him no childish terror, nor even wonder; all seemed so peaceful and natural. It was only later, as he grew older, that he learnt Death's inner meaning.

The account he gave me of his own life in early childhood was as follows:—

I was very lonely—that was the chief feature of my childhood—I was very lonely. I saw my father seldom: he was away a great deal, but his presence pervaded the whole house and was one of the deepest influences on my life. I was kept in the charge of servants of the household after my mother died, and I used to sit, day after day, in front of the window and picture to myself what was going on in the outer world.

From the very first time that I can remember, I was passionately fond of Nature. Oh! it used to make me mad with joy when I saw the clouds come up in the sky one by one. I felt, even in those early days, that I was surrounded with a companionship very intense and very intimate, though I did not know how to name it. I had such an exceeding love for Nature, that I cannot think in what way to describe it to you; but she was a kind of loving companion, always with me, and always revealing to me some fresh beauty.

This was how he pictured his childhood to me on that foggy day in London, and a passage in his *Reminiscences* makes the portrait still more vivid:—

In the morning of autumn (he writes) I would run into the garden the moment I got up from sleep. A scent of leaves and grass, wet with dew, seemed to embrace me, and the dawn, all tender and fresh with the newly awakened rays of the sun, held out its face to me to greet me beneath the trembling vesture of palm-leaves. Nature shut her hands and laughingly asked every day: "What have I got inside?" and nothing seemed impossible.

II

Rabindranath Tagore went on to tell me that his first literary awakening came from reading the old Bengali poets, Chandidas and Vidyapati. He studied them in a recently published edition, when he was twelve or thirteen, and revelled in their beauty. He went still further, and, with the precocity of youth, imitated their style and published some poems under the name of Bhanu Sinha. Literary Bengal wondered for a time who this Bhanu Sinha could be. He laughed as he told me of this exploit of his boyhood, and went on to say that these and many other juvenile poems were merely conventional and imitative. They followed the old classical style.

When he wrote, however, the poems published later under the name of *Sandhya Sangit* (Evening Songs), he broke away from the classical style altogether and became purely romantic. At first he was derided by the older generation for his new metres; but the younger generation was with him. He chose no English model; the early Vaishnava religious literature was the source of his inspiration. These religious poems ever afterwards remained intimately endeared to him. Their influence is marked in his own lyrics, and especially in the *Gitanjali* series.

III

The time of his real birth as a poet he dates from a morning in Free School Lane, Calcutta, when with dramatic suddenness the veil seemed to be withdrawn from his eyes and he saw the inner soul of reality.

It was morning (he said to me). I was watching the sunrise from Free School Lane. A veil was suddenly withdrawn and everything became luminous. The whole scene was one perfect music—one marvellous rhythm. The houses in the street, the men moving below, the little children playing, all seemed parts of one luminous whole—inexpressibly glorious. The vision went on for seven or eight days. Everyone, even those who bored me, seemed to lose their outer barrier of personality; and I was full of gladness, full of love, for every person and every tiniest thing. Then I went to the Himalayas, and looked for it there, and I lost it. . . . That morning in Free School Lane was one of the first things which gave me the inner vision, and I have tried to explain it in my poems. I have felt, ever since, that this was my goal: to express the fullness of life, in its beauty, as perfection—if only the veil were withdrawn.

I copied this account down as the Poet told it on that dark, misty London morning; and I can remember distinctly even now the quiet laugh he gave as he said, "And I lost it," and also the emphasis he laid upon the words "fullness of life." In Rabindranath's own prose writings the same incident is also recorded. It may be well to compare this other record with the picture he gave me in London. They corroborate and explain one another.

Where the Sadar Street ends, trees in the garden of Free School Street are visible. One morning I was standing in the verandah, looking at them. The sun was slowly rising above the screen of their leaves; and as I was watching it, suddenly, in a moment, a veil seemed to be lifted from my eyes. I found the world wrapt in an inexpressible glory with its waves of joy and beauty bursting and breaking on all sides. The thick shroud of sorrow that lay on my heart in many folds was pierced through and through by the light of the world, which was everywhere radiant.

That very day the poem known as *The Fountain Awakened from its Dream* flowed on like a fountain itself. When it was finished, still the curtain did not fall on that strange vision of beauty and joy. There was nothing and no one whom I did not love at that moment. . . . I stood on the verandah and watched the coolies as they tramped down the road. Their movements, their forms, their countenances seemed to be strangely wonderful to me, as if they were all moving like waves in the great ocean of the world. When one young man placed his hand upon the shoulder of another and passed laughingly by, it was a remarkable event to me. . . . I seemed to witness, in the wholeness of my vision, the movements of the body of all humanity, and to feel the beat of the music and the rhythm of a mystic dance.

For some days I was in this ecstatic mood. My brothers had made up their minds to go to Darjeeling, and I accompanied them. I thought I might have a fuller vision of what I had witnessed in the crowded parts of the

Sadar Street, if once I reached the heights of the Himalayas.

But when I reached the Himalayas the vision all departed. That was my mistake. I thought I could get at truth from the outside. But however lofty and imposing the Himalayas might be, they could not put anything real into my hands. But God, the Great Giver, Himself can open the whole Universe to our gaze in the narrow space of a single lane.

IV

The volume of lyrics called *Morning Songs* was the direct outcome of this time of ecstatic early vision. There is a romantic longing to know intimately the secret of the beauty of the world. But as yet he had not the deep-laid basis of practical experience whereon to build. His first lyrics, therefore, are mainly in the realm of imagination, and not closely related to common human experience.

But outer circumstances, as well as his own inner spirit, prevented the young writer from remaining too long in that enchanted garden of the soul. His father, seeing his son's remarkable genius, very wisely insisted that he should leave Calcutta and go down to the banks of the Ganges in order to supervise there the family estate. This work brought him into closest touch with the village life of Bengal. He had to deal each day with the practical affairs of men, and to understand and appreciate the elemental hopes and fears of mankind, stripped of all convention. To his own good fortune, also, as a poet, his joy in communing with Nature found at the same time its fullest and freest expression. During pauses in his active business life he would live all alone on the sand-flats of the Ganges, moving up and down from village to village in his boat.

Sometimes (he told me) I would pass many months absolutely alone without speaking, till my own voice grew thin and weak through lack of use. I used to write from my boat the stories of the village life which I had witnessed in the course of my work, and put into written words the incidents and conversations which I had heard. This was my "short-story" period; and some think these stories better than the lyrics which I had written before.

It was during this long residence at Shileida that the deepest love for Bengal, his motherland, developed. The national movement had not yet come into actual outward shape and form; but the forces which were to break forth later were already acting powerfully in the hearts of leading Bengali thinkers; and Rabindranath's soul caught the flame of patriotism, not in Calcutta itself, but among the villagers. His unshaken faith in the destiny of his country received its strongest confirmation from what he saw in the village life of his own people. He was not unaware of the dangers which threatened that life through its contact with the new social forces from the West. Indeed, this forms the theme of many of his short stories. But he believed, with all his heart, from what he had witnessed, that the stock from which the new national life was to spring forth was sound at the core. He spoke to me, that morning, with the greatest possible warmth and affection of the Bengali villagers, and of the many lessons he owed to them of patience and simplicity, of human kindliness and sympathy.

V

Rabindranath Tagore dated the next stage in his literary life from the time when he went to Santiniketan Asram from Shileida.

He left his father's estate; and there seemed to come to him the strongest impression that a new period of adventure was about to arrive in his life. He anticipated some change, for which these quiet unbroken years in the country had been a preparation.

Slowly there came to him the clear call to give up his life more wholly for his country. He first went to Calcutta in order to found a school, and afterwards to Santiniketan with the same object. On his arrival at Santiniketan, to take up this new work, he was handicapped for want of funds. "I sold my books," he said to me pathetically.

I sold all my books, my copyrights, everything I had, in order to carry on the school. I cannot possibly tell you what a struggle it was, and what difficulties I had to go through. At first the object in view was purely patriotic, but later on it grew more spiritual. Then, in the very midst of all these outer difficulties and trials, there came the greatest change of all, the true *Varsha Sesha*,[1] the change in my own inner life.

He went on to tell me how, when he was forty years old, his wife had died, and almost immediately after his daughter showed signs of consumption. He left the school and went away with his daughter to nurse her and tend her, but after six months of mingled hope and fear she passed away from his arms and left his heart still more desolate. Then came the third overwhelming wave of sorrow. His youngest son, to whom he had learnt to be father and mother in one, was taken suddenly ill with cholera and died in his presence —the child of his love.

As he spoke of these things that morning, the darkness of the London mists rolled away and the light shone through the clouds with a majestic radiance. This outward scene was but a faint symbol of the story that was being told me so quietly in that upper room.

The Poet spoke of the days and hours wherein Death itself became a loved companion—no longer the king of terrors, but altogether transformed into a cherished friend.

You know (he said to me), this death was a great *blessing* to me. I had through it all, day after day, a sense

[1] Lit., "The end of the old year."

of fulfilment, of completion, as if nothing were lost. I felt that if even an atom in the universe seemed lost, it could never actually perish. It was not mere resignation that came to me, but the sense of a fuller life. I knew then, at last, what Death was. It was perfection.

Through what depth of suffering that peace and joy came out at last triumphant, the lines in his face told me as he spoke these words.

VI

It was during this period that *Gitanjali* was written in his own mother-tongue, Bengali. "I wrote," he said, "those poems for myself. I did not think of publishing them when I was writing."

They mark the great transition in his life, when the Poet's social and national longings became wholly merged in the universal. He has attempted —to use his own words—"to express the fullness of human life, in its beauty, as perfection."

Since that period of sorrow he has fared forth as a voyager, a pilgrim. This is the last phase of all. It was his own health which first compelled him to set out to the West. But here again, as in the former period mentioned, the outward circumstance has brought with it a new spiritual development.

As I crossed the Atlantic (he wrote to me), and spent on board ship the beginning of a new year, I realized that a new stage in my life had come, the stage of a voyager. To the open road! To the emancipation of self! To the realization in love!

In another letter, which he wrote earlier to me, dealing with the meeting of the conflicting races of the world and the removal of colour prejudice, he uses these words:—

This meeting of the races affords the greatest of all problems that men have ever been asked to solve. It is, I believe, the one question of the present age, and we must be prepared to go through the martyrdom of suffering and humiliation till the victory of God in man is achieved.

Since *Gitanjali* was written, Rabindranath Tagore has been facing, day by day, these larger international questions and casting aside altogether that narrower nationalism which for one period in his life had affected his own songs. He has attempted, also, to comprehend the inner harmony of his own life's work and to read its deeper meaning. The stage of philosophy has been reached by the Poet. Yet his lyrical powers seem in no way to be diminished. The fountain of song is still sending forth new streams.

VII

When Rabindranath Tagore first landed in London, in 1912, he had placed before his English friends some translations of his Bengali poems.

He had offered them with singular diffidence, without at all realizing the value of his great achievement. "I found," he said, "that I had to strip my Bengali verses of all their gaudy ornaments and to clothe them in the simplest English dress."

That English setting has since been acknowledged, by those who are best able to judge, to represent a beautiful and musical prose—a comparatively new form of English, which has enriched the literature of Great Britain. The triumph has been won—a triumph hardly ever before achieved in literary history—of an author translating his own poems into a wholly new language, thus giving his message to two peoples at once in a noble literary form.

This crowning success of Rabindranath Tagore has already brought East and West closer together in a common fellowship and understanding. Where the forces of racial rivalry and religious division are so strong, it is indeed no small blessing to humanity when a generous voice can be clearly heard, above the discordant tumult of the times, which the whole world welcomes as a messenger and revealer of peace and good will to mankind.

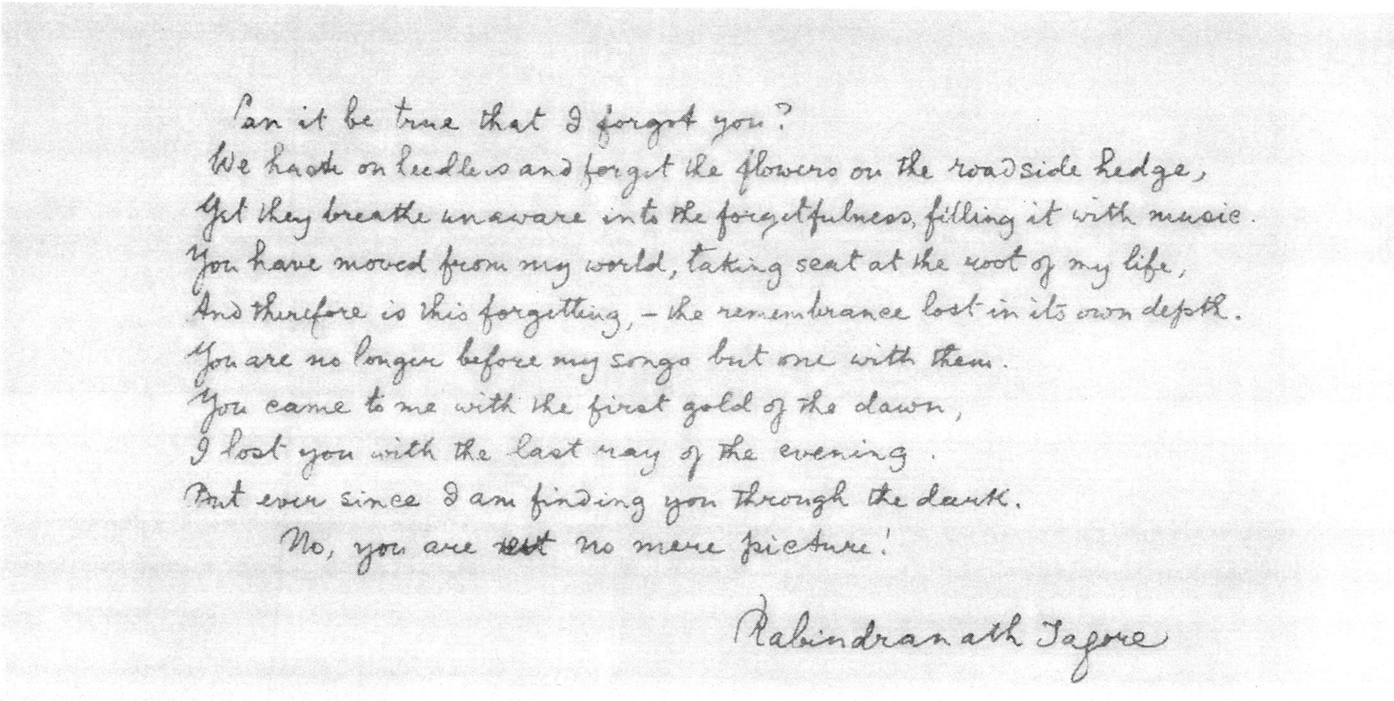

Can it be true that I forgot you?
We hasten on heedless and forget the flowers on the roadside hedge,
Yet they breathe unaware into the forgetfulness, filling it with music.
You have moved from my world, taking seat at the root of my life,
And therefore is this forgetting, — the remembrance lost in its own depth.
You are no longer before my songs but one with them.
You came to me with the first gold of the dawn,
I lost you with the last ray of the evening.
But ever since I am finding you through the dark.
No, you are no mere picture!

Rabindranath Tagore

Facsimile of the poet's hand writing

A LIST OF INDIAN PLACES, WORDS, AND PHRASES WITH THEIR MEANING

Places.	*Meaning.*
Bolpur . .	A small town and railway station near Santiniketan.
Padma . .	The main branch of the Ganges as it reaches the delta in Bengal.
Santiniketan	Literally the "Abode of Peace"—the name of the religious retreat (or Asram) where the poet Rabindranath Tagore usually dwells. It was founded by his father, Maharshi Debendranath Tagore.
Shileida . .	The village on the Padma where the Poet's country house is situated.
Surul . .	A village near Santiniketan. The important agricultural work in connection with the Asram is carried on at Surul.
Uttarayan .	The house of the Poet at Santiniketan—so called because it lies to the north of the Asram.
Vichitra . .	The hall of music and art in the Poet's house at Calcutta.
Visva-bharati	"World Culture." The name given to the higher educational work in the Poet's Asram, which is of an international character.

Sanskrit Texts.	*Meaning.*
"Asato ma sad Gamaya" .	"Lead me from untruth to truth."
"Pita No'si"	"Thou art our Father."
"Santam, Sivam, Advaitam"	"The Peaceful, The Good, The One."

Sanskrit Words.	*Meaning.*
Ahimsa . .	Non-violence—the opposite to *himsa*, or violence.
Amrita . .	That which is immortal.
Ananda . .	Joy.
Asram . .	A religious retreat.
Brahma Vidya	The knowledge of God.
Mantram . .	A sacred Sanskrit text.
Maya . . .	Illusion.
Mukti . .	Salvation, or spiritual freedom.

NARAYAN . .	God manifest in man.
NIRVANA . .	Cessation from misery through extinction of desire.
RUPAM . .	Form.
SANYASI . .	An ascetic.
SATYAGRAHA .	Truth-force, or Soul-force.
SATYAM . .	The True.
TAPASYA . .	Commonly translated "penance." An endeavour to reach spiritual fulfilment through sacrifice and concentration of powers.
TAPOVANA .	A forest retreat for spiritual realization.
Miscellaneous.	*Meaning.*
VINA . . .	A famous stringed instrument of India.
TAMBURA . .	A very simple stringed instrument used for repeating the key-note.
EKTARA . .	A one-stringed instrument used by wandering minstrels.
BANDE MATARAM	"Hail, Motherland!"—the national cry of modern India.
BAUL . . .	A sect of religious mendicants, who sing in the villages of Bengal.
FIRST OF BAISAK . .	The New Year's Day in Bengal, which comes about April 13th or 14th.
MADHAVI . .	Jasmine.
PANCHAYAT .	Committee.
SAL . . .	A tree with very beautiful foliage.
SANTAL . .	An aboriginal tribe, living near the Asram.
SARI . . .	A single piece of cloth, about five yards long and four feet wide, with which women drape themselves.
SEVENTH PAUS FESTIVAL	The anniversary celebration, held about December 21st each year.
SWARAJ . .	Self-government.

NOTE.

THE letter *s* in Bengal is pronounced soft, and is almost equivalent to "Sh." Thus "Santiniketan" must be pronounced in English as "Shantiniketan"; "Asram" as "Ashram"; "Visva-bharati" as "Vishwa-bharati." The spelling of these words is not always consistent. Sometimes the aspirate is added, and sometimes it is omitted. The vowels in Bengali and Sanskrit should be pronounced in the Italian manner.

LETTERS TO A FRIEND

CHAPTER I

THE letters contained in this opening chapter were written to me by the poet Rabindranath Tagore in the early years when my work as teacher at Santiniketan had only just begun. He came back from Europe in September 1913, but I was not able to join him then on account of an attack of malarial fever. Later on it was necessary for me to go out to South Africa along with my friend W. W. Pearson in order to take part in the Passive Resistance struggle which was being carried on against the evils of the indenture system of Indian labour. We both returned to India in April 1914, and were with the Poet until we went out to Fiji together in September 1915.

Some explanation must be given concerning the special series of letters which the Poet sent me each day from Ramgarh, near Naini Tal, in the latter part of May 1914.

He had gone in good health to the Hills in order to spend there his summer holidays; but he told me afterwards that the mental pain he experienced soon after his arrival was almost equivalent to a death-agony. He had hardly expected to survive it. This was all the more strange because it came upon him quite suddenly at a moment when he was feeling a sense of physical exhilaration in the supreme beauty of the Himalayas and also the delight of the change from the intense heat of the plains. I remember him saying to me that the shock of agony overtook him like a thunderstorm out of a clear, unclouded sky.

This suffering, which is referred to in the letters written in May, entirely passed away. The Poet was in the best of health and spirits all through the month of June, renewing his own full, active work in his school among his boys after the holidays were over. Indeed, I can remember June 1914 as a singularly happy month.

But early in July the darkness again came down upon his life and seemed once more to overwhelm him. It appeared to have no external source, either in bad health or bad climate; and the school work was progressing wonderfully. But he spoke to me constantly of the mysterious and unbearable weight of mental oppression which drove him into solitude. He went away from the school and lived alone at Surul. For nearly three months this depression continued. There are hardly any letters written during this period; but I have the most vivid and painful recollections of his suffering.

Long before any news reached us about the World War that was impending, and before any hint of it had come to us in the midst of our comparative retirement from the world at Santiniketan, his mind was entirely preoccupied with the foreboding of some disaster which was about to overwhelm humanity. He wrote at this time, and published some weeks before the war began, a very remarkable Bengali poem called *The Destroyer*, in which he spoke of the sudden destruction that was coming upon the earth. It contained the following lines:—

Is it the Destroyer who comes?
For the boisterous sea of tears heaves in the flood-tide of pain.
The crimson clouds run wild in the wind, lashed by lightning, and the thundering laughter of the Mad is over the sky.
Life sits in the chariot crowned by Death.
Bring out your tribute to him of all that you have.

Looking back now on that period, when humanity was suddenly torn in pieces by internecine war, it seems certain to me that the Poet's highly sensitive nature had made him feel dimly beforehand the tragedy which was about to happen. In no other way can I account for his intense mental suffering.

LONDON, *August 16th*, 1913

I am so glad to know that you are now in Santiniketan. It is impossible to describe to you my longing to join you there.

The time has come at last when I must leave England;

for I find that my work here in the West is getting the better of me. It is taking up too much of my attention and assuming more importance than it actually possesses. Therefore I must, without delay, go back to that obscurity where all living seeds find their true soil for germination.

This morning I am going to take a motor-ride to Rothenstein's country house, and if I delay any longer I may not have time to write to my other correspondents by this mail, so I must close this letter.

CALCUTTA, *October 11th*, 1913

I have gone through a period of difficulty. My life had appeared to me lonely and burdened with responsibilities too heavy for a single man to bear. Evidently my mind has got into a habit of leaning too much upon my friends whom I had acquired in England, and letting most of its current flow outward. Therefore, coming to my own country, where the contact of humanity is not so close as in the West, I felt suddenly stranded and in a desolation, wherein every individual has to struggle through his own problem unaided. For some length of time, solitariness weighed upon my heart like a heavy load, till I gained my former mental adjustment and felt again the current turn inward from the world outside. Now I feel the flood-tide of life and companionship. It sweeps the burden from off my shoulders and carries me along with it on its joyous course.

In India the range of our lives is narrow and discontinuous. This is the reason why our minds are often beset with provincialism. In our Asram at Santiniketan we must have the widest possible outlook for our boys, and universal human interests. This must come spontaneously—not merely through the reading of books, but through dealings with the wider world.

SANTINIKETAN, *October 11th*, 1913

You must certainly rid your system of this malarial poison before you take up your regular work at Santiniketan.

Is it wholly impossible for you to come down here at once, and stay with us quietly and indulge in absolute rest for some time? Jagadananda had a very bad type of malaria before he joined his work here. His coming to Bolpur has been the saving of his life. Do give our Asram a trial. She will nurse you back to health. Your room shall be fitted with a desk and writing materials and other necessaries. You can start a little gardening in our school grounds and take occasional excursions into our *Sal* grove. Possibly, giving me a Greek lesson now and then will not fatigue you too much, if you feel so inclined.

Just now the singing mood is upon me, and I am turning out fresh songs every day.

SANTINIKETAN, *February* 1914

(*Written to meet me in England after my return from South Africa*)

I send you my love and the translation of a song of mine written about two months ago. We are waiting for you, knowing that you are coming to us with your heart filled with the wisdom of death and the tender strength of sorrow.[1] You know our best love was with you, while you were fighting our cause in South Africa along with Mr. Gandhi and others.

My days of turmoil are not yet over. Indeed, I have not yet been able to settle down to my work and to my

[1] Referring to the death of my mother, which took place while I was in South Africa.

rest. Interruptions come almost daily to me in various forms. At last I have made up my mind to be rude, and to leave all invitations ignored and letters unanswered.

The mango blossoms have appeared in our Asram. The air is full of music, heard and unheard, and I do not know why we should be callous to the call of the seasons and foolishly behave as if the Spring and the Winter are the same to human beings, with the same round of works to follow, without having the option to be occasionally useless and absurd. However, I am in that mood when one forgets that he has any other obligations to meet than to be good for nothing and glad.

SANTINIKETAN, *March 5th*, 1914

Lately I have been spending some days alone in the solitude of Shileida; for I needed it very greatly, and it has done me good. I feel that I must protect myself from all distractions for some time, so as to be able to add to my inner resources, never considering it a duty to force myself to work merely with the vain intention of doing good, but rather making the work I do living and real.

To try to benefit others, and yet not to have enough of oneself to give others, is a poor affair.

SANTINIKETAN, *May 10th*, 1914

When are you coming to stay with me in the Hills? I am afraid you are passing through a great deal of worry, and you are in need of a good rest. I won't let you work during this vacation. We must have no particular plans for our holidays. Let us agree to waste them utterly, until laziness proves to be a burden to us. Just for a month or so we can afford to be no longer useful members of society. The cultivation of usefulness produces an enormous amount of failure, simply because in our avidity we sow seeds too closely.

RAMGARH, *May 14th*, 1914

Here I feel that I have come to the place that I needed most in all the world. I hated to be disloyal to the plains of Bengal, where the earth lies so meek and unobtrusive, leaving the sky to the undisputed dominion of all the horizons. But happily the poet's heart is inconstant; it is easily won; and to-day I am already bending my knees to Father Himalaya asking pardon for keeping aloof for so long in blind distrust.

The hills all round seem to me like an emerald vessel brimming over with peace and sunshine. The solitude is like a flower spreading its petals of beauty and keeping its honey of wisdom at the core of its heart. My life is full. It is no longer broken and fragmentary.

RAMGARH, *May 15th*, 1914

At last I am supremely happy, not simply because the quiet of this place affords me the needful change from the worries of a crowded life, but because it supplies my mind with its natural food. Directly I come to a place like this I can realize at once that I had been living before on half-rations.

I have found myself since I came here, and I am filled with the wonder that the infinite Power and Joy has become what I am and what this blade of grass is. When we are restless we raise dust all about us and we forget the supreme truth that "we are." I cannot tell you the great joy of seeing everything through the sight which comes from within.

RAMGARH, *May 17th*, 1914

To-day is my father's birthday anniversary. We have just had our morning prayer, and my mind is full. It is a stormy morning, dark and threatening, with an occasional burst of pallid light. It seems like the symbol of a spiritual new birth. I have been experiencing the feeling of a great expectation, although it has also its elements of very great suffering. To be born naked in the heart of the eternal Truth; to be able to feel with my entire being the life-throb of the universal heart—that is the cry of my soul. I tell you all this, so that you may understand what I am passing through and may help me when the occasion arrives.

Do take care of yourself and get well, so as to be fit to fight your own battle with renewed strength and hope.

RAMGARH, *May 21st*, 1914

I am struggling on my way through the wilderness. The light from across the summit is clear; but the shadows are slanting and deep on the slope of the dark valley. My feet are bleeding, and I am toiling with panting breath. Wearied, I lie down upon the dust and cry and call upon His name.

I know that I must pass through death. God knows, it is the death-pang that is tearing open my heart. It is hard to part with the old self. One does not know, until the time comes, how far it had spread its roots, and into what unexpected, unconscious depths it had sent its thirsty fibres draining out the precious juice of life.

But the Mother is relentless. She will tear out all the tangled untruths. We must not nourish in our being what is dead. For the dead is death-dealing. "Through death lead us to deathlessness." The toll of suffering has to be paid in full.

For we can never enter the realm of white light and pure love until all our debts are cleared and nothing binds us to the dead past. But I know my Mother is with me and before me.

RAMGARH, *May 22nd*, 1914

The spiritual bath is not that of water, but of fire. For the water merely takes away the dirt that is superficial, not the dead matter that clings to life, abusing its hospitality. So we must take our plunge into fire, time after time.

We shrink and tremble at the prospect; but the Mother assures us that it will never touch anything that is true and living.

The fire consumes the sin, but not the soul. Our soul is the last thing that we come to know; for it is dark where the Mother feeds the soul in secret. And we can see that sacred sight in the intense glow of the fire of suffering. Sometimes Death brings the torch to light it, and sometimes a messenger whose face is hidden from us.

The latter is at my door. I ask him questions. He answers not. But the fire is burning fiercely, exposing the hidden corners of my being with all their unsuspected accumulations of untruth and self-deception. Let the fire burn until it has nothing to feed upon. Let nothing be spared that awaits destruction.

RAMGARH, *May 23rd*, 1914

Now I feel that I am emerging once again into the air and light and am breathing freely. It is an unspeakable relief to come out into the open and the normal, to regain the balance of life once more, to be able to take again my natural part in the open fair of the world.

Strenuousness is the open foe of attainment. The strength that wins is calm and has an exhaustless resource in its passive depth. Greed is sure to frustrate itself, even the greed after God.

I had been struggling, during these last few days, in a world where shadows held sway and right proportions were lost. The enemies with whom I was fighting were mostly phantoms. But this experience of the dark has had a great lesson for me. Untruth when spread thinly over a large area of life is hardly felt and seen. We live in truce with it. Now that I have had its vision, in all its concentrated ugliness, I am called upon to fight it every day of my life.

RAMGARH, *May 24th*, 1914

To-day I feel as sound as these mountain oaks, ready to store my share of light from the sky and joyfully try my strength with the storm when it comes. Again I feel that I must have all my interests alive, grow on all sides, and enter into various relations with the world, keeping my body and mind fully awake.

Harmony is difficult when one's own nature is complicated; when the strings in the *vina* are numerous and each one claims its right to be tuned.

But I know life is simple, however complex the organism may be; and everything goes to pieces when the living truth of the central simplicity is lost.

RAMGARH, *May 25th*, 1914

Morning is simple, though infinitely more varied than night; for it is open and luminous. Night tries to hide and suppress all problems of reality, making the tyranny of dreams absolute. Light bares the heart of truth; and whatever is unformed or struggling, dying or dead is revealed, not merely at the side but at the root of all that is growing in strength and grace.

We see all the contradictions, yet we feel the inner harmony; strife and struggle are everywhere, yet beauty is supreme. This makes Night, with its phantoms of false mystery and exaggeration, slink away in shame when Morning appears in her simple robe of white. Hope and joy come in her wake all the more triumphant, because not a single blade of grass or thorn is hidden. Morning has dawned upon me at last. My wrestlings with the shadows are over. My heart looks out upon the undulating field of life, chequered with the fruitful green and the pallor of the sandy waste, and feels that all is good. It is vast; it is free to all the horizons; and over it from end to end reigns the light of the sky.

CHAPTER II

THE period of the next few months was one of increased tension, followed later by a gradual recovery from the mental strain that had been oppressing the Poet for so long.

At the beginning of the European War this strain had become almost unbearable, owing both to the world tragedy of the war itself and the suffering of Belgium, which the Poet felt most acutely. He wrote and published simultaneously in India and England three poems which expressed the inner conflict going on in his own mind. The first of these was called *The Boatman*, and he told me, when he had written it, that the woman in the silent courtyard, "who sits in the dust and waits," represented Belgium. The most famous of the three poems was *The Trumpet*. The third poem was named *The Oarsmen*. Its outlook is beyond the war; for it reveals the daring venture of faith that would be needed by humanity if the old world with its dead things were to be left behind and the vast uncharted and tempestuous seas were to be essayed leading to a world that was new.

A fourth poem, which was not published then, but later, was given to me by the Poet towards the end of the year 1914. On Christmas Day that year he delivered in the Asram a very remarkable address to the students and teachers, speaking of Christ, who was called the Prince of Peace, and how the name of Christ was being denied in Europe.

SANTINIKETAN, *October 4th*, 1914

It seems as though I am coming out of the mist once more, and I am trying to throw off my shoulders the burden that has been oppressing me all these days. As my mind feels lighter, I hope I have rightly earned my freedom.

We have all come to Santiniketan from Surul; and this change has done me good. Dr. Maitra has sent me a long letter about you. He thinks you will have to be very careful in future about your health, if you are not to get ill again.

SANTINIKETAN, *October 7th*, 1914

My period of darkness is over once again. It has been a time of very great trial to me, and I believe it was absolutely necessary for my emancipation. I know that I am being lifted from the sphere where I was before; and it is the loneliness of the new situation and the cry of the old life that is still troubling me. But I have glimpses of the ineffable light of joy, which I am sure will not fail me. Preaching I must give up, and also trying to take up the rôle of a beneficent angel to others. I am praying to be lighted from within, and not simply to hold a light in my hand.

DARJEELING, *November 11th*, 1914

Real love is always a wonder. We can never take it for granted. Your love for me I accept with joy and thankfulness, and wonder to which account to put it. Perhaps every man has some worth unknown to himself, inspiring love through the cover of his self. It gives one a hope that truth is more than appearance, and that we deserve more than we can claim with apparent reason. Love is for the unlimited in us, not for the one who is loudly evident.

Some say that we idealize him we love; but the fact is that we realize through love the ideal in him—and the ideal is the real, if we know it. We have the eternal contradiction in us, that our worth unfolds itself through our unworthiness, and love can go beyond the process, overtaking the ultimate truth. We could never be certain that we are more in truth than we are in fact, if we were not loved.

Give my love to Mr. Rudra. Tell him I am hopelessly lost in the wilderness of correspondence, distributing thanks to all quarters of the globe, till not an atom of gratitude is left in my nature.

CALCUTTA, *November 12th*, 1914

I know these school financial difficulties are good for us, but I must have strength enough to extract the good. We must have faith in the Truth. But this faith must be active and self-respecting. The whole Asram must rouse itself from its passive inanity and be ready to meet the danger, never expecting help from outside, but using all its wisdom, self-restraint and resourcefulness.

Our school is a living body. The smallest of us must feel that all its problems are his own; that we must give, in order to gain. Even the little boys should not be kept entirely ignorant of our difficulties. They should be made proud of the fact that they also bear their own share of the responsibility.

CALCUTTA, *November 15th*, 1914

Critics and detectives are naturally suspicious. They scent allegories and bombs where there are no such abominations. It is difficult to convince them of our innocence.

With regard to the criticism of my play, *The King of the Dark Chamber*, that you mention in your letter, the human soul has its inner drama, which is just the same as anything else that concerns Man, and Sudarshana is not more an abstraction than Lady Macbeth, who might be described as an allegory representing the criminal ambition in man's nature. However, it does not matter what things are, according to the rules of the critics. They are what they are, and therefore difficult of classification.

Ramgarh is said to be not unfavourable for wintering; and this it is that has induced me to try to go there for quiet during the next few months till it becomes decently warm and comfortable. But it is a secret of mine, and you must not let it out. Whatever may happen, I must remain beyond the reach of correspondence. I need to be entirely alone. By going to an inaccessible region, I shall escape anniversary meetings, addresses and conferences, and other evils that the flesh is *not* heir to, but which, all the same, fasten upon it without ceremony. It is wicked of me to be away when you are returning to the Asram after your illness; but I feel that you will have a better opportunity of coming closer to the boys and teachers if I am not there, and that will compensate you for my absence.

AGRA, *December 5th*, 1914

I was surprised to read in the *Modern Review* that our Bolpur boys are going without their sugar and ghee in order to open a relief fund. Do you think this is right? In the first place, it is an imitation of your English schoolboys and not their own original idea. In the second place, so long as the boys live in our institution they are not free to give up any portion of their diet which is absolutely necessary for their health. For any English boy, who takes meat and an amount of fat with it, giving up sugar is not injurious. But for our boys in Santiniketan, who can get milk only in small quantities, and whose vegetable meals contain very little fat ingredients, it is mischievous.

Our boys have no right to choose this form of self-sacrifice—just as they are not free to give up buying books for their studies. The best form of self-sacrifice for them would be to do some hard work in order to earn money; let them take up menial work in our school—wash dishes, draw water, dig wells, fill up the tank which is a menace to their health, do the building work. This would be good in both ways. What is more, it would be a real test of their sincerity. Let the boys think out for themselves what particular works they are willing to take up without trying to imitate others.

ALLAHABAD, *December 18th*, 1914

I feel happy to imagine you lost in the sunny blue and the silent green of our Asram, and I am glad that we have had our talk together before you left. I know from my own experience that our Asram will give you the peaceful detachment of mind needed so much for bringing oneself face to face with one's own inner being and the deeper reality of the world.

You must have recognized by this time that I have something elusive in me, which eludes myself not less than others. Because of this element in my nature, I have to keep my environments free and open, fully to make room in my life for the Undreamt-of who is expected every moment. Believe me, I have a strong human sympathy, yet I can never enter into such relations with others as may impede the current of my life, which flows through the darkness of solitude beyond my ken. I can love, but I have not that which is termed by phrenologists "adhesiveness"; or to be more accurate, I have a force acting in me, jealous of all attachments, a force that ever tries to win me for itself, for its own hidden purpose.

If this purpose were only moral, it could be more easily tolerated—nay, welcomed; but it is life-purpose—the purpose of growth—and for this very reason it meets with a certain amount of opposition when it crosses with other life-currents. It may seem to be egoistic. But this life-impulse I speak of belongs to a personality which is beyond my ego. I must own this Master in me, who is not a mere abstract moral ideal, but a Person. I must be true to it, even at the cost of what men call happiness, at the risk of being misunderstood, forsaken and hated. I am sociable by nature, and would intensely like to enjoy the company of friends, the pleasures and advantages of friendship. But I am not free to give myself away, even when it seems necessary and good; and the somewhat wide expanse of time and space that I always try to keep in reserve about me is not mine to use as I wish. This loneliness often becomes hard for me to bear, but I have my ample compensation; and I dare say it will bear fruit for those who know what to expect from it.

The human soul is God's flower. It gives its best bloom and scent, not when shut up in eager palms to be squeezed, but when left alone in the immense freedom of light and air. But, very unfortunately,

> The World is too much with us; late and soon
> Getting and spending, we lay waste our powers;
> Little we see in Nature that is ours;
> We have given our hearts away, a sordid boon!

My love is bare and reticent. It was gaudily covered in its youthful flowering season; bulging with gifts in its fruitful maturity; but now that its seed-time has come, it has burst its shell and is abroad in the air; it has thrown away all the extra burden of allurements, carrying in its minute covering the density of its life. So when you come and shake the bough for it, it will not answer; for it is not there. But if you can believe in its silence, and accept it in silence, you will not be disappointed.

The following is the translation of the Bengali poem given to me by the Poet at Christmas, 1914:—

JUDGEMENT

When, mad in their mirth, they raised dust to soil thy robe,
O Beautiful, it made my heart sick.
I cried to thee and said: "Take thy rod of punishment and judge them."
The morning light struck upon those eyes, red with the revel of the night; the place of the white lily greeted their burning breath; the stars through the depth of the sacred dark stared at their carousing—at those that raised dust to soil thy robe, O Beautiful!
Thy judgement-seat was in the flower garden; in the birds' notes in springtime; in the shady river banks, where the trees muttered in answer to the muttering of the wave.

O my Lover, they were pitiless in their passion.
They prowled in the dark to snatch thy ornaments to deck their own desires.
When they had struck thee and thou wert pained, it pierced me to the quick, and I cried to thee and said: "Take thy sword, O my Lover, and judge them!"
Ah, but thy justice was vigilant.

A mother's tears were shed on their insolence; the imperishable faith of a lover hid their spears of rebellion in its own wounds.
Thy judgement was in the mute pain of sleepless love; in the blush of the chaste; in the tears of the night of the desolate; in the pale morning light of forgiveness.

O Terrible, they in their reckless greed climbed thy gate at night, breaking into thy storehouse to rob thee.
But the weight of their plunder grew immense, too heavy to carry or to remove.
Thereupon I cried to thee and said: "Forgive them, O Terrible!"
Thy forgiveness burst in storms, throwing them down, scattering their thefts in the dust.
Thy forgiveness was in the thunderstone, in the shower of blood; in the angry red of the sunset.

CALCUTTA, *January 20th*, 1915

I could feel from your last letters, hastily written, that you were depressed. Your mind is still in that region of phantoms where shadows are exaggerated and the least thing makes one unhappy. I find that your very happiness is a strain to you—it is so jerky and violent—because very often it comes to you in the shape of reaction. It makes me feel far more anxious about you than your bad health.

CALCUTTA, *January 29th*, 1915

I don't like to frighten you with news of my ill-health, but it must be given to justify my absence from the Asram. I feel that I am on the brink of a breakdown. Therefore I must take flight to the solitude of the Padma. I need rest and the nursing of Nature.

If you ever have a relapse of your illness, do not despair. Try not to fret, or to strain, but to give yourself up to sleep. We must not force ourselves to be too conscious, even of God—our spirit cannot bear it. Depression comes very often from repletion. Our subconscious nature must have sufficient time to store up what our conscious nature requires.

CALCUTTA, *January 31st*, 1915

I hear that you are really ill. This won't do. Come to Calcutta. Consult some doctor; and if he recommends, come to Shileida, where I am going to-morrow morning. I dare not go to Bolpur. I have reached such a sublime depth of tiredness, that it has conferred a dignity on my selfish isolation; and I don't feel the least ashamed of my flight from all responsibilities. I must be alone, with all my heart and soul.

But you must not delay. We are very anxious about you, and we cannot let you break down completely.

SHILEIDA, *February 1st*, 1915

You are right. I had been suffering from a time of deep depression and weariness. But I am sane and sound again, and willing to live another hundred years, if critics would spare me. At that time I was physically tired; therefore the least hurt assumed a proportion that was perfectly absurd. However, I am glad that there is still the child in me, who has its weakness for the sweets of human approbation. I must not feel myself too far above my critics. I don't want my seat on the daïs; let me sit on the same bench with my own audience and try to listen as they do. I am quite willing to know the healthy feeling of disappointment when they don't approve of my things; and when I say "I don't care!" let nobody believe me.

A great proportion of our humankind is inarticulate. I find I have quite a number of friends among them, and that I need not put any bounds to my estimation of their partiality towards my writings; so that though they do not confirm, neither do they contradict.

I am living in a boat here in a lovely spot. Mukul, Nandalal and another artist are my companions. Their enthusiasm of enjoyment adds to my joy. Every little thing brings to them a sense of surprise, and thus their fresh minds come to my service, bringing to my notice things that I have been getting into the habit of ignoring.

SHILEIDA, *February 3rd*, 1915

Directly I reached here I came to myself, and am now healed. The cure for all the illness of life is stored in the inner depth of life itself, the access to which becomes possible when we are alone. This solitude is a world in itself, full of wonders and resources unthought of. It is so absurdly near, yet so unapproachably distant. But I do not want to talk; please forgive my absence and my silence. I cannot afford to scatter my mind just now.

I do so earnestly hope that you are better.

CALCUTTA, *February 18th*, 1915

Calcutta will keep me till Sunday. I do not expect to free myself from its clutches before then, though I shall try. Anyhow, Monday will see me in Bolpur, somewhat feeble and worn-out, unfit to be trusted with any responsibility.

I hope that Mahatma and Mrs. Gandhi have arrived in Bolpur, and Santiniketan has accorded them such a welcome as befits her and them. I shall convey my love personally to them when we meet.

I am glad that our Asram has given shelter to the persecuted Rajput boy. Let him feel that he has won a home in Santiniketan by being driven from his own place and by his own people.

CHAPTER III

In the middle of the month of May 1915, after repeated illnesses from which I had hardly recovered, an attack of Asiatic cholera came suddenly upon me, which proved very nearly fatal. The Poet himself helped to nurse me, and his care and affection were full of the most sensitive tenderness and sympathy. On my account, he did not go away for a holiday during the worst of the hot weather. He waited near at hand, while I was slowly recovering in a nursing-home in Calcutta. At last, when I was able to be moved to Simla, as a convalescent, his letters began again.

During this year 1915 we were so completely outside the range and area of the war, in our isolation in India itself, that its horrors gradually tended to recede into the background of our minds; but the greater thoughts which had been awakened so painfully during the previous year, owing to the war itself—such as the problem of human suffering; the possibility of complete human brotherhood; the meeting of East and West in common fellowship—these were more present than ever before. Our talks together, while I was in the nursing-home in Calcutta, were continually about these problems. They remained deep in the subconscious mind of the Poet all through this year. At the same time, the whole burden of the school work at Santiniketan fell upon his shoulders and he threw himself into every detail of it with his own characteristic energy and determination.

Through the summer of 1915 the Poet's plans were maturing for a visit to the Far East. His father, Maharshi Debendranath Tagore, had made his Far Eastern journey more than half a century before, and it had formed one of the means by which he had realized so deeply in his own life the universal brotherhood of man. To the Poet, whose thoughts were always in the terms of Humanity rather than in those of any lesser unit, the fratricidal war in the West revealed the dangerously unbalanced condition of the human race. Out of the agony from which he had suffered in the previous year, both before and after the war had begun, the determination had been ever growing in his own mind to enlarge the bounds of his Asram at Santiniketan, which his father, the Maharshi, had founded as a home of religion. He looked more and more to the time when his Asram would pass beyond the school stage and become a centre of world fellowship, wherein students and teachers from the East and West should be equally honoured and welcomed.

These thoughts were brooding in his mind during the year 1915; therefore it became clear to him that a visit to the Far East, in order to win the friendship and co-operation of the leading thinkers of China and Japan, would be necessary if the cycle of his work at Santiniketan was to be completed. He had very nearly made up his mind to start in August, and had actually taken his passage on a Japanese steamer, when a series of circumstances intervened which made the journey impossible.

After these plans for a voyage to the Far East had been entirely abandoned, a sudden crisis arose in India itself with regard to a humanitarian struggle against the indentured system of Indian labour in the colonies. My friend W. W. Pearson and I had fully investigated and condemned this system in Natal, and we were therefore more immediately in touch with the direct problem than other people. The immoral and servile conditions of indentured Indian labour had to be thoroughly exposed. For this reason, after the tour to the Far East had been abandoned, we received the Poet's cordial consent, when we proposed to go out together to Fiji and carry through an independent inquiry into the indenture system of Indian labour in that colony. He felt very keenly indeed that this new journey of ours would be in keeping with his own ideals of universal brotherhood and fellowship, and he gave us his blessing on our departure. Two texts from the Upanishad were his own gift to me when we bade him farewell.

They may be translated as follows:—

From Joy all things have their origin: in Joy they subsist, and unto Joy they return.

I meditate upon His glory, who creates the earth, the sky and the stars, and sends into our minds the power of comprehension.

The inspiration which Rabindranath Tagore thus gave to us, by his encouragement and sympathy, carried us through what proved to be the most difficult journey we had ever undertaken. In the end, the inquiry we made very nearly effected its object; and the pledge was given that the whole indenture system of Indian labour would be abolished at the earliest possible moment.

SANTINIKETAN, *June 30th*, 1915

Just now I am in Santiniketan. It still has the holiday atmosphere; for only a few boys have come back, and it is not unlikely that some of them have left for good. So our Finance Minister will have a hard time before him with arrears to clear off and the buildings to complete. Do not try to come now, however strong you may feel—for financial difficulties are just as bad as disease germs in their insidious attacks on our health. However, be assured that this bad time will not be thrown away on us altogether, and we shall come out of it with more freedom than ever, if considerably thinner.

As for myself, I have the call of the open road, though most of the roads are closed. I am in a nomadic mood, but it is becoming painful to me for want of freedom. I am carrying, as it were, my tents on my back, instead of living in them.

Possibly my life is on the eve of another bursting of

its pods and scattering of its seeds; there is that continual urgency in my blood, the purpose of which is hidden. The conclusion is being forced upon me that poets should never bind themselves to any particular work; for they are the instruments of the world's moods. And after the years of building up all kinds of benevolent schemes, my life is emerging once again upon the open heath of irresponsibility, where the sun rises and sets, where there are wild flowers, but no committee meetings.

CALCUTTA, *July 7th*, 1915

Haven't I confessed elsewhere that renunciation is not for me, and that my freedom is to be moving from bondage to bondage? My mind must realize itself anew. Once I give form to my thought, I must free myself from it. For the time being, it seems to me that I want absolute freedom to create new forms for new ideas. I am sure physical death has the same meaning for us—the creative impulse of our soul must have new forms for its realization. Death can continue to dwell in the same sepulchre, but life must unceasingly outgrow its dwelling-place; otherwise the form gets the upper hand and becomes a prison. Man is immortal; therefore he must die endlessly. For life is a creative idea; it can only find itself in changing forms.

Forms are stupid dumb things, that struggle to stand still, until at last they break into pieces.

You will have heard about all my plans from Pearson. I am seeking my freedom by surrendering my ideas into the hands of a new bondage. In Santiniketan, some of my thoughts have become clogged by accumulations of dead matter. I do not believe in lecturing, or in compelling fellow-workers by coercion; for all true ideas must work themselves out through freedom. Only a moral tyrant can think that he has the dreadful power to make his thoughts prevail by means of subjection. It is absurd to imagine that you must create slaves in order to make your ideas free. I would rather see them perish than leave them in the charge of slaves to be nourished. There are men who make idols of their ideas, and sacrifice humanity before their altars. But in my worship of the idea I am not a worshipper of Kali.

So the only course left open to me, when my fellow-workers fall in love with the form and cease to have complete faith in the idea, is to go away and give my idea a new birth and create new possibilities for it. This may not be a practical method, but possibly it is the right one.

CALCUTTA, *July 11th*, 1915

Conscientious men are comfortable men; they live within the bounds of their duties, and consequently enjoy their fixed proportion of leisure. But I shirk my duties in order to create works that eat up all my time; and then I suddenly leave my work and try to elope with unmitigated indolence.

I shall be floating on the Padma before the next week is out, and shall forget to imagine that my presence in the Council of Creation is imperatively necessary for the betterment of Humanity. I am a born nomad—as I am sure you are—and my work has to be fluid, if it is to be my work. But absolute fluidity in work can only be had at its commencement. Therefore my duty is to start things and then leave them. Unless I leave them and keep at a distance, I cannot help them in maintaining their ideal character. But, this time, it is the fatigue of my body and mind that is driving me into solitude. The kind of work that I can do in a particular scheme requires freshness of mind more than perseverance. Therefore there must be a break before I resume my duties.

It is easy for me to understand the stress of pain that

you are feeling now about the wrongs of the world, and especially among the weaker races of mankind, who are oppressed by the strong. Human wrongs are not pitiable, they are terrible. Those who are in power forget every day that it is for their very power's sake that they have to be just. When God's appeal comes from the weak and the poor, then it is full of danger for those who are in power; for then they are apt to think that they can disregard it with impunity, especially if it upsets their office arrangements in the very least degree. They have more faith in their pitiful system and their prestige than in moral providence.

In India, when the upper classes ruled over the lower, they forged their own chains. Europe is closely following Brahmin India, when she looks upon Asia and Africa as her legitimate fields for exploitation. The problem would be simpler if she could altogether denude other continents of their population; but so long as there are alien races, it will be difficult for Europe to realize her moral responsibility with regard to them. The gravest danger is when Europe deceives herself into thinking that she is helping the cause of humanity by helping herself; that men are essentially different, and what is good for her people is not good for others who are inferior. Thus Europe, gradually and imperceptibly, is losing faith in her own ideals and weakening her own moral supports.

But I must not go on weaving truisms; and on our own side I must equally acknowledge this truth, that weakness is heinous because it is a menace to the strong and the surest cause of downfall for others than those who own it. It is a moral duty for every race to cultivate strength, so as to be able to help the world's balance of power to remain even. We are doing England the greatest disservice possible by making it easy for her to despise us and yet to rule; to feel very little sympathy for us and yet to judge us.

Will Europe never understand the genesis of the present war, and realize that the true cause lies in her own growing scepticism towards her own ideals—those ideals that have helped her to be great? She seems to have exhausted the oil that once lighted her lamp. Now she is feeling a distrust against the oil itself, as if it were not at all necessary for her light.

SHILBIDA, *July 16th*, 1915

I wonder whether you got my last letter, which I wrote to you in a railway train, informing you of my proposed visit to Japan.

I am busy floating my dreams, as the children do their paper boats, on this wide expanse of green, gold and blue. This world is wonderfully beautiful, but you cannot help feeling that there is a lurking pain in its heart, which has its own immortal beauty. It is a pearl shell of wonderful tints and design, hiding in its bosom a tear-drop, which gives it priceless value. All our payments have to be made in pain; otherwise life and this world would become cheap as dirt.

SHILEIDA, *July 23rd*, 1915

After long years I have come among my tenants; and I feel, and they also, that my presence was needed. It was a great event of my life when I first dwelt among my own people here, for thus I came into contact with the reality of life. For in them you feel the barest touch of humanity. Your attention is not diverted, and then you truly know that Man is very much to man. One is apt to forget them, just as one does not think of the earth on which one walks.

But these men compose the great mass of life, which sustains all civilizations and bears their burdens. They are content barely to live, so that others may prove that man's life is a great deal more than mere existence. They keep steady the level of the minimum, which is enormous quantitatively, so that the maximum may be unhampered by its own development. Thousands of acres of land are tilled, so that a University can be maintained upon one acre. Yet these men are insulted merely because while they are so absolutely necessary, it is their necessity to live that drives them to this position. They are in their place because they cannot help it.

We all hope that here, at this very point, Science in the end will help man. She will make the necessities of life easily accessible to every man, so that humanity will be freed from the tyranny of matter which now humiliates her. This struggling mass of men is great in its pathos, in its latency of infinite power. It is beautiful where it is simple and spontaneous; sublime where it is large, deep and enduring. I must confess that I have been neglecting these people, while I was away from them in Santiniketan; and I am glad that I am now with them once more, so that I may be more actively mindful of them. I am afraid my life at the Asram was at last making me into a teacher, which was unsatisfactory for me, because unnatural. But one has to be a helper to be a real man; for then you share your life with your fellow-beings and not merely your ideas.

CALCUTTA, *July 29th*, 1915

The Infinite Being is not complete if He remains absolutely infinite. He must realize Himself through the finite; that is, through creation. The impulse to realize comes from the fullness of joy; but the process must be through pain. You cannot ask why it should be—why the Infinite should attain truth by passing through the finitude; why the joy should be the cause of suffering, in order to come back to itself—for it is so. And when our minds are illumined, we feel glad that it is so.

When we fix all our attention to that side of the Infinite where it is pain and death, where it is the process of fulfilment, we are overwhelmed. But we must know that there is the positive side; that always there is a completeness along with the incomplete. Otherwise, there would be no pity in us for the suffering; no love in us for the imperfect.

What I am trying to express is this: you saw the monkey dead entangled in the telegraph-wires, while round it was beauty in all its superbness. The incongruity struck you as cruel. That is something. The cruelty would not have been apparent to you if ugliness were absolute. You felt the pity of it, because there is the ideal of perfection. Here, in this ideal, lies our hope and the ultimate solution of our doubts. In creation, joy is always getting the better of pain, otherwise our sympathy for pain would be unmeaning.

Then why should we despair? We cannot fathom the mystery of existence. But this much we have known, that there is a love which is greater in truth than pain and death. Is not that sufficient for us?

SANTINIKETAN, *August 7th*, 1915

Your letter was of great interest to me. I have one principle to guide my thoughts in most things of vital importance. It is this, that the figure which represents creation is not "one," but "two." In the harmony of two contradictory forces everything rests. Whenever our logic tries to simplify things, by reducing the troublesome "two" into "one," it goes wrong. Some philosophies say that motion is all *maya* and truth is static;

others are of the opinion that truth is fluid and it is only *maya* that represents truth to us as static.

But truth is beyond logic; it is the everlasting miracle; it is static and dynamic at the same time; it is ideal and real; it is finite and infinite.

The principle of war and that of peace both make truth. They are contradictory; they seem to hurt each other, like the finger and the strings; but this very contradiction produces music. When only one predominates, there is the sterility of silence. Our problem is not only whether we should have war or peace, but how to harmonize them perfectly.

So long as there is such a thing as force, we cannot say that we must not use force, but rather that we must not abuse it, as we are prone to do when we make it the sole standard and ignore love. When love and force do not go together, then love is mere weakness and force is brutal. Peace becomes death when it is alone. War becomes a demon when it destroys its mate.

Of course, we must not think for a moment that killing one another is a necessary form of war. Man is pre-eminently on a moral plane, and his weapons should be moral weapons.

SANTINIKETAN, *September 23rd*, 1915

(*Written on the eve of our departure to Fiji*)

The golden bell of the autumn sun tolls silently and the period for migration has come. You and Pearson are the first of our brood who have left their nest for the passage across the seas; and I can hardly control my wings. Things round us have their weight, and they gradually sink into our soul without our knowing it, till one day we are oppressed with a burden whose nature we hardly know. Movement is the only cure when life becomes heavy with *débris*.

My heart at this moment is like a leaky boat, full of water, that can just keep itself afloat, but the least burden of responsibility becomes too much for it. I must go to the wilderness and take upon myself the severe discipline of freedom. I want to say "No" emphatically to all the importunities of the world; to all the moral and social obligations. But in spite of my protestations, I am afraid that I shall have to end my days as an ascetic—with certain modifications.

I am going on with the rehearsal, and rather like it. For it gives me opportunity to come close to the little boys, who are a perpetual source of pleasure to me.

CHAPTER IV

After our return from Fiji, at the end of January 1916, the longings of the Poet to go out to the Far East became insistent. He took W. W. Pearson, Mukul Dey the artist and myself with him on this voyage. We sailed from Calcutta on the *Tosa Maru*. In the Bay of Bengal our vessel passed through a terrible cyclone and had great difficulty in weathering the storm. Our stay in China was very short, because the people of Japan were impatiently waiting for the Poet's arrival in their own country. They received him with enthusiasm at first, as one who had brought honour to Asia.

But when he spoke out strongly against the militant imperialism which he saw on every side in Japan and set forward in contrast his own ideal picture of the true meeting of East and West, with its vista of world brotherhood, the hint went abroad that such "pacifist" teaching was a danger in war-time, and that the Indian Poet represented a defeated nation. Therefore, almost as rapidly as the enthusiasm had arisen, it subsided. In the end, he was almost isolated, and the object for which he had come to the Far East remained unfulfilled. It was at this time that he wrote his poem called *The Song of the Defeated*, which begins:—

My Master bids me, while I stand at the wayside,
to sing the song of defeat.
For that is the bride whom He woos in secret.

These summer months in Japan, at a time when the fever of militarism was at its height, were filled with disappointment. The mental suffering which had appeared at the beginning of the war returned. The Poet's whole inner nature was in revolt against the violently aggressive spirit of the age. All this is brought out in his book called *Nationalism*, the first chapters of which were written in Japan at a white heat. These lectures, delivered in Japan, were reprinted in Europe. They were translated into French in Switzerland by Romain Rolland towards the end of the year 1916. It needs to be added that at a later visit to Japan, in 1924, these earlier impressions, formed in war-time, were considerably modified. He found then in Japan, as also in China, those who were eager to appreciate his universal message.

The Poet went from Japan to America, accompanied by W. W. Pearson and Mukul Dey, while I returned to the Asram. His stay in America was crowded with engagements. He made new friends and received great kindness at their hands. In many ways he was satisfied with his visit, and felt that it had been a success. But he fell ill there, and after a short time came back home by way of the Pacific, only staying between steamers in Japan and China.

Shortly after his arrival at the Asram it became necessary for me to go out again to Fiji, in order to obtain the final and complete abolition of the indenture system of Indian labour. The years 1917 and 1918 were fully taken up by the Poet with quiet fruitful work at Santiniketan. All the while, his plans for widening the scope and aim of his educational enterprise, after the war was over, were slowly shaping themselves in his mind. These will come forward as the main subject in the succeeding chapters in this book; for they began to absorb his whole attention.

After returning from Fiji, early in the year 1918, I was free to remain at the Asram. Since I was constantly with the Poet from that time onwards, I received no letters from him, but some which he sent to W. W. Pearson in England may serve to keep touch with his thoughts up to the close of this period.

SRINAGAR, KASHMIR. *October 12th*, 1915

I am technically in Kashmir, but still have not entered its gate. I am passing through the purgatory of public receptions and friendly solicitations; but Paradise is in sight. Now I feel I am coming nearer myself; the intruder in me, who always fusses about arranging and dusting his absurd store of knicknacks, is, I hope, shut out at least for a few weeks. It is becoming easier for me to feel that it is I who bloom in flowers, spread in the grass, flow in the water, scintillate in the stars, live in the lives of men of all ages.

When I sit in the morning outside on the deck of my boat, before the majestic purple of the mountains, crowned with the morning light, I know that I am eternal, that I am *ananda-rupam.*[1] My true form is not that of flesh or blood, but of joy. In the world where we habitually live, the self is so predominant that everything in it is of our own making and we starve because we have to feed upon ourselves. To know truth is to become true; there is no other way. When we live the life of self, it is not possible for us to realize truth.

"Come out, come away." This is the urgent cry we have in our soul—the cry in the blood of the chick, living in its shell. It is not merely truth that frees us, but freedom that gives us truth. That is why Buddha dwelt on the importance of freeing our lives from trammels of self; for then Truth comes of itself.

Now I understand at last that the restlessness that has been so persistent with me is of this nature—I must come out from the life of habit, the life of compromise, the life of self. I think the first step towards it is going to the solitude.

My coming to Kashmir has helped me to know clearly what I want. It is likely that it will become obscured again when I go back to my usual routine; but these occasional detachments of life from the usual round of customary thoughts and occupations lead to the final freedom—the Santam, Sivam, Advaitam. The first stage towards freedom is the Santam, the true peace, which can be attained by subduing self; the next stage is the Sivam, the true goodness, which is the activity of the soul when self is subdued; and then the Advaitam, the love, the oneness with all and with God.

---

[1] Literally " Joy-Form." This is a part of a famous Sanskrit text.

Of course this division is merely logical; these stages, like rays of light, may be simultaneous or divided according to the circumstances, and their order may be altered, such as the Sivam leading the Santam. But all we must know is that the Santam, Sivam, Advaitam, is the only goal for which we live and struggle.

SHILEIDA, *February* 3, 1916

Coming away from Calcutta, I have come to myself. Every time it is a new discovery to me. In the town, life is so crowded that one loses the true perspective. After a while it makes me feel weary of everything, simply because the truth of our own self is lost sight of. We have our Lover waiting in the depth of our being. Unless we come to him, time after time, the tyranny of things grows intolerable. We must know that our greatest resource of all is lying hidden in our heart. We have to be assured of it in order to be cured of our miserliness.

SHILEIDA, *February 5th*, 1916

You know the English translation of my poem about "taking truth simply." Last night, while reading it in *The Gardener* along with others, it seemed to me strangely incongruous in its semi-metrical form. It was like meeting a woman dressed in tights in the midst of others dressed in simple *saris*. So I tried to divest it of its metrical disguise, though it is difficult to exorcise altogether the ghost of the old metre.

Whatever may come, my heart, take truth simply,
Though there be some who can love you, there must be others who never can, and if you must know the cause, it is as much in you as in them, and in all things around.

Some doors are closed against your knocks, while your doors are not open always and to all comers.
Such has been and shall be for evermore; and yet if you must have peace, my heart, take truth simply.

There is no need to be abusive if your boat founders by the shore, though it sailed through the storm.
Keep yourself afloat by all means; but if it is impossible to do so, then be good enough to sink without noise.
It is a commonplace fact that things may or may not fit you and events happen without asking for your leave.
Yet if you must have peace, my heart, take truth simply.

You press and are pressed hard in the crowd, but space there is enough and to spare in this world.
When you have counted your losses to the last farthing, your sky remains as blue as ever.
You find, when suddenly tested, that to live is sweeter than to die.
You may miss this and that and the other thing, but if you must have peace, my heart, take truth simply.

Must you stand with your back to the rising sun and watch your shadow lengthened before you?
Must you take pleasure in finding fault with your destiny and thus tease your soul to death?
Then for mercy's sake be quick and have done with it; for if, with the evening stars, you must light your lamp, my heart, take truth simply.

SHILEIDA, *February 24th*, 1916

Where are you? Seven fathoms deep in your report-writing? When are you going to float up into the sun and sail on, dancing with all surface-drifts of existence?

I have my work here, but it is play as well. It does not savour of office and officials; it has its humour and some amount of pathos. It is almost like painting a picture.

Pearson has succeeded in getting ill and joining me on my trip.

SANTINIKETAN, *July 9th*, 1917

This is the first time that you have given me your address in your letter since your departure for Fiji. We have been feeling very anxious since we learnt about your accident and injury to your back and leg.

The boys have begun their agriculture in right earnest under the leadership of Santosh Mitra; and I believe it is not going to be like the road—the brilliant work of Nepal Babu—which suddenly stops, with a sublime futility, at the brink of Nowhere. The artist Surendranath Ker has joined our school, and his presence is very much appreciated by the boys and the teachers. Our former student and a veteran of Calcutta football fields, Gora, has taken up the work of a mathematical teacher, and I am sure he will prove to be a valuable acquisition to us.

The rainy season this year, like a great many of our boys, did not wait until the vacation was over, but made its appearance before the time and has been very seriously attending to its business ever since. I have taken my seat of indolence at the window of my second storey—in the middle region between the extravagant pageantry of the clouds and the immense spread of the exuberant green of the earth.

There was a time when my life seemed to be an overflow of spendthriftness in a reckless Universe, before Purposefulness crept into the Eden Garden of my youth and changed the naked felicity of existence into the draped decency of a fashionable cut. I am waiting to regain that Lost Paradise of mind, to forget that I must be of any use to anybody, and to know that the true purpose of my life is the great purpose in me of All-time and All-world, urging me to be fully what I am.

And am I not a poet? What business have I to be anything else? But unfortunately I am like an inn, where the poet lodger has to accommodate strange bedfellows by his side. Yet is it not high time for me to retire from this none too lucrative business of the innkeeper? Anyway, I am feeling tired, and my duty to my numerous lodgers is in imminent danger of being shamefully neglected.

SHILEIDA, *July 20th*, 1917

The accompanying letter is from Pearson. I am glad that he has come out of his seclusion feeling better in mind and body.

After a separation of nearly a year and a half, I have come once more to my Padma and have renewed my courtship. She is unchanged in her changeableness. She is shifting her course and leaving the side of Shileida. She is showing a decided preference for Pabna. My only consolation is that she cannot remain constant for long.

It is a beautiful day to-day. The sunshine is coming out after the fitful showers of rain, like a boy emerging from his dive in the sea with his naked limbs glowing and glistening.

CALCUTTA, *March 6th*, 1918

(*The letters that follow were written to W. W. Pearson*)

Each one of us in this unfortunate country is looked upon with suspicion, and our British rulers cannot see us clearly through the dust which they themselves raise. Humiliation follows us at every step and in each good work we try to do.

All blind methods are easy methods at the beginning. But such cheap methods as these do not pay in the end. For, after all, mere bullying is stupidity; it assumes frightfulness only because it does not know its way. What is radically wrong with our rulers is this: they are fully aware that they do not know us, and yet they do not *care* to know us. And, in consequence, thorny hedges are springing up of unscrupulous intermediaries between the rulers and the ruled, giving rise to conditions which are not only miserable, but unspeakably vulgar.

I have just received a letter from Thadani, complaining of the insults and harassments which only Indian British subjects have to go through in British ports. These have the effect of making them feel ashamed of the Government under which they live. Such invidious treatment is sinking deeply into the memory of my people, and the moral providence of history cannot altogether ignore such an accumulated burden of indignities loaded upon humanity.

SANTINIKETAN, *March 10th*, 1918

I can guess from your letter that some questions are troubling your mind about the best way of self-realization. There can be no single path for all individuals; for we vastly differ in our natures and habits. But all great masters agree in their teaching on one cardinal point, saying that we must forget our personal self in order to attain our spiritual freedom. Buddha and Christ have both of them said that this self-abnegation is not something which is negative—its positive aspect is love.

We can only love that which is profoundly real to us. The larger number of men have the most intense feeling of reality only for themselves; and they can never get out of the limits of their self-love. The rest of mankind can be divided into two classes—those who have their love for persons and those who have their love for ideas.

Generally speaking, women fall into the first category and men into the second. In India this fact has been recognized. Therefore our teachers have pointed out two different paths for the two different sexes.

It has been said that women can attain their emancipation by sublimating their personal relationships into the realm of the ideal. If, in spite of all obvious contradictions, a woman can realize in her husband something which transcends his personal limitations, then through her devotion to him she touches the Infinite and thus is freed from the bondage of self. Through the luminous intensity of her love, her husband and her child reveal to her the ultimate Truth which is divine. For biological reasons, men's natures have had comparative freedom from the attachment to persons, and therefore it has become easier for them to find direct access to those ideas, lying behind the screen of things, which they have ever been pursuing in all their knowledge and creative activities. Once you become conscious of the idea, as the inner spirit of reality, the joy becomes so unbounded that your self becomes obliterated, and you can easily lay aside all that you have for its sake.

But we must keep in mind that love of persons and love of ideas can both be terribly egoistic, and therefore may lead to bondage instead of setting us free.

It is only constant sacrifice in service which can loosen the shackles. We must not merely enjoy our love (whether personal or ideal) by contemplating its beauty and truth, but rather make it fruitful by giving expression to it in our life's work. Our life is the material whereby we have to build the image of the ideal of Truth that we have in our mind. But life, like all other materials, contains an obstinate antagonism to the idea to which it must give shape. Only through the active process of creation can such antagonism be discovered at every step and chiselled away at every stroke.

Look at the aboriginal Santal women around our Asram. In them the ideal of physical life finds perfect development only because they are ever active in giving it expression in work. Their figures and their movements attain their beautiful harmony because they are always being tuned by life's activities. The one thing which I am never tired of admiring is the vigorous cleanliness of their limbs, which never get soiled even by the constant contact with dirt. Our ladies, with their soaps and scents, only give an artificial polish to the superficial body; but the cleanliness which is induced by the body's own current of movement, coming from the completeness of physical health, can never be theirs.

The same happens with regard to our spiritual body. It is not by meticulous care in avoiding all contaminations that we can keep our spirit clean and give it grace, but by urging it to give vigorous expression to its inner life in the very midst of all the dust and heat.

But I must stop to find out if I have given in what I have written any answer to the original question you have put to me. It may be that I have not; for it is difficult to know exactly what you want of me. You have spoken of impersonal love and impersonal work, and you ask me which I consider to be the greater. To me, they appear as one, like the sun and the light; for love's expression is in work. Where love has no work, there is a dead world.

SANTINIKETAN, *October 6th*, 1918

All through this last session in the Asram, I have been taking school classes in the morning and spending the rest of the day in writing text-books. It is a kind of work apparently unsuitable for a man of my temperament.

Yet I have found it not only interesting but restful. The mind has its own burden, which can be lightened when it is floated on a stream of work. Some engrossing ideas also help us in the same way. But ideas are unreliable; they run according to no time-table whatever; and the hours and days you spend in waiting for them grow heavy.

Lately I have come to that state of mind when I could not afford to wait for inspiration of ideas; so I surrendered myself to some work which was not capricious, but had its daily supply of coal to keep it running. However, this teaching was not a monotonous piece of drudgery for me; for I have been treating my students as living organisms; and any dealing with life can never be dull.

Unfortunately, poets cannot be expected to enjoy lucid intervals for long. Directly some new subject takes possession of their minds, they become useless for all decent purposes. They are intellectual gypsies; vagrancy is in their blood; and already I feel the call of the irresponsible vagabondage, a kind of passion for extravagant idleness. The schoolmaster in me is perilously near being lured away by the mischievous imps of truancy.

I am going to move away from this place in a day or two, with the ostensible reason of visiting South India, from where invitations have been pouring in upon me for a long time; but I tell you in confidence, it is the lapse of reason—my frequent visitor—the Spirit of Truancy, that is beckoning me, ready to escort me over all lines of proscribed works. I long to discover some fairy-land of holidays—not a lotus-land—not a world where all weekdays are Sundays—but where Sundays are not at all needed, where all works carry their rest in themselves, where all duties look delightfully undutiful, like clouds bearing rain, appearing perfectly inconsequential.

SANTINIKETAN, *December 11th*, 1918

Yesterday I had a letter from the University of Sydney asking me if it was true that I would not visit Australia, even if I was wanted there. I have written, in answer, that it would be wrong on my part if I refused to accept any invitation sent in the right spirit. Pride of patriotism is not for me. I earnestly hope that I shall find my home anywhere in the world, before I leave it. We have to fight against wrongs, and suffer for the cause of righteousness; but we should have no petty jealousies or quarrels with our neighbours merely because we have different names.

The barrier of Self is *maya*. When it is dispelled, then we in our suffering have tasted the draught of sorrow that wells up from the heart of creation, flowing out to be merged and transformed into the sea of endless joy.

When we do not see ourselves in the Infinite, when we imagine our sorrow to be our very own, then life becomes untrue and its burden becomes heavy. I understand more and more the truth of Buddha's teaching, that the root of all our miseries is this self-consciousness. We have to realize the consciousness of the All before we can solve the mystery of pain and be free.

Our emancipation lies through the path of suffering. We must unlock the gate of joy by the key of pain. Our heart is like a fountain. So long as it is driven through the narrow channel of self it is full of fear and doubt and sorrow; for then it is dark and does not know its end. But when it comes out into the open, on the bosom of the All, then it glistens in the light and sings in the joy of freedom.

Rabindranath Tagore

From the dry point by Mukul Dey

CHAPTER V

THE letters that now remain to be quoted form an almost uninterrupted series, though I have continued to divide them into chapters. They were written by the Poet during a long tour, in Europe and America, in which he was accompanied by his friend W. W. Pearson.

Out of the misery and darkness of the Great War, Rabindranath Tagore had been led, step by step, to the one fixed purpose of gradually forming at Santiniketan Asram a home of brotherhood and peace, where East and West might meet in a common fellowship of study and work.

At first his design had been to gather together at his Asram the scattered religious cultures of Asia in order to present them in a united manner to the rest of the world. But his comprehensive vision could not stop at any horizon that was less wide than humanity. During the years 1918 and 1919 he took me with him on many tours, while he wandered up and down India, seeking to find a seed-ground in which his thoughts concerning human progress might take root in the soil and afterwards bear fruit. I was able to watch in these tours this one central purpose that I have mentioned taking concrete shape. He pictured to himself Santiniketan opening its doors to the whole world, and inviting those who were lovers of peace and good will, in East and West alike, to come together there, on equal terms, without distinction of caste or race or creed.

He named the institution which should offer such world-hospitality Visva-bharati. "Visva" in Sanskrit means "world,"—in its universal aspect. "Bharati" is more difficult to translate, but implies knowledge, wisdom, culture. Visva-bharati was to be a House of Learning for all peoples and all religions.

The Poet traced back his whole conception to the Upanishads and had in his mind those forest Asrams, or religious retreats, of ancient India, which were freely open to all who came to them, and made their guests welcome with the fullness of fellowship and love. One of the most celebrated of his lectures was called "The Religion of the Forest." In a noble passage from another lecture he concludes with the following words:—

"Our forefathers spread a single pure white carpet, whereon all the world was cordially invited to take its seat in amity and good-fellowship. No quarrel could have arisen there; for He in whose name the invitation went forth, for all time to come, was Santam, Sivam, Advaitam—the Peaceful, in the heart of all conflicts; the Good, who is revealed through all losses and sufferings; the One, in all diversities of creation. And in His name was this eternal truth declared in Ancient India:—

He alone sees truly who sees all beings as himself."

For the fulfilment of his central purpose it was necessary for him to go once more to Europe and America in order to gain the support of the West and to invite the West to his Asram. But at the very time when he was beginning to prepare for his journey certain disturbances occurred in the Punjab which for a time threw everything else into the background. Riots had occurred and reprisals had been taken. At the critical moment when the news came about Amritsar I happened to be with him in Calcutta, and it will be impossible for me ever to forget the torture of his mind. Night after night was passed sleeplessly. At last some relief came to him by renunciation of his knighthood as a protest against what had been done. For a time it seemed as though "Amritsar" had shattered all his hopes and aims.

But while he felt such intense sensitiveness, as a poet, at the wrong which had been done to humanity in Jallianwalla Bagh, he took his stand at once against any memorial being erected upon the spot as a permanent record of the deed of blood. In the same way, on an earlier occasion, when asked in Japan to celebrate, by means of a short poem, to be engraved on a rock, a tragic story concerning a blood-feud, he wrote:—

They hated and killed, and men praised them,
But God in shame hastened to hide its memory under
the green grass.

I have mentioned these facts because they belong essentially to the period covered by the letters which follow. They reveal the inner spirit of the Poet as at last, after long absence, he approached Europe in the year 1920. With a great effort he had recovered his serenity of mind. His faith in the generous spirit of the West had passed through its ordeal of fire. Deep down in his subconscious nature he had been wounded at heart by the events of the previous year in the Punjab. Therefore it was with great anxiety that I watched his vessel depart from Bombay, and went back to the Asram.

RED SEA, *May 24th*, 1920

We shall reach Suez this evening. It is already beginning to grow cold, and now I feel that we have reached a truly foreign part of the world under the rule of different gods than ours. Our hearts are strangers in this region and even the atmosphere of this place looks askance at us. The people here want us to fight their battle and supply them with our raw materials, but they keep us standing outside their doors, over which is written on the notice-board: "Trespassers from Asia will be prosecuted." When I think of all this, my thoughts shiver with cold and I feel home-sick for the sunny corner in my Santiniketan bungalow.

To-day is Monday, and next Sunday morning our steamer will reach Marseilles. But I am already counting the days for my return journey; and I know the sight of the bare rocks of Aden will give a thrill of delight to my heart while pointing with lifted fingers the way to India.

LONDON, *June 17th*, 1920

Time is scarce, and sugar, and butter, and a quiet place where I can gather thoughts and recognize myself. Do not expect long letters from me, or indeed anything else. The fury of social engagements is on me. It is a thing on which one might compose an Ode like that on the West Wind. I am willing to try, if only it would allow me some time to do it. The poet Hafiz was willing to exchange the wealth of Samarkand and Bokhara for a mole on the cheek of his beloved. I am willing to give the whole of London away for my corner in Santiniketan. But London is not mine to dispose of; neither was the wealth of Samarkand and Bokhara the Persian poet's. So our extravagance does not cost us anything, nor does it bring us any help.

I am going to Oxford to-morrow. Then I shall be knocking about in different places. Just at this moment I am starting for a tea-party given in my honour, from which I cannot absent myself on any pretext, unless I can manage to be run over by a motor-car in the London streets. It is a matter of eternal wonder to me that this does not happen to me four times a day. You won't believe in my scarcity of time if I go on to the end of the note-paper. So I hastily bid you farewell.

LONDON, *July 8th*, 1920

Every day I have been wishing to write you a letter—but the flesh is weak. My days have become solid like cannon-balls, heavy with engagements. It is not true that I have no leisure at all, but unfortunately I cannot utilize interrupted leisure for any work whatever. Therefore those intervals are lost doing nothing.

I am sure you know it, better than anybody else, that doing nothing is a burden hard to bear. But if you look at my exterior, you will find no trace of damage there—for my health is absurdly good.

I hope Pearson is regularly furnishing you with all the news. He has been of very great help to me, as you can well imagine, and I find that the arduous responsibility of looking after a poet suits him wonderfully well. He is looking the very picture of health, and on the whole his dreams are felicitous. For instance, last night he dreamt that he had been buying strawberries as large as gourds. It proves the magnificent vitality of his dreams.

I know our school vacation is over. The boys are back at school and the Asram is resounding with laughter and song. The advent of the rains is also contributing its portion to the general rejoicing. How I wish I had wings! Give my love to all the children, and my blessings.

LONDON, *July 12th*, 1920

It gave me great joy, and a feeling of relief, when your sister came to see me yesterday and gave me reassuring news about your other sister. She repeatedly asked me to tell you that there was not the least cause for anxiety on account of them, and that they were comfortably settled in their new home. I gave her all the news about you, but unfortunately could not assure her that you were careful of your own health.

Invitations are pouring in from the continental countries, and I feel sure that a hearty welcome is awaiting me in these places. When I am weary and feel a longing to go back, it gives me strength to think that the migratory flock of my thoughts have found their nest on these shores, and with genuine love and wonder these enormously busy people have listened to a voice from the distant East.

This is a constant surprise to me. However, there is no question that one only truly and fully lives where one's thoughts and works find their medium of responsive life.

When I am in the West, I feel more strongly than ever that I am received in a living world of mind. I miss here my sky and light and leisure, but I am in touch with those who feel and express their need of me and to whom I can offer myself.

It is not unlikely that some time hence my thoughts will no longer be necessary to them and my personality will lose its flavour; but does it matter? The tree sheds its leaves, but the fact is that so long as these were living they brought sunshine into the heart of the tree and their voice was the voice of the forest; and my communication with Western humanity has been a communication of life. Even when it ceases, the fact remains that it brought some rays of light there, which have been transformed into the living stuff of their minds. Our span of life is short and opportunities are rare, so let us sow our seeds of thought where the soul claims them and where the harvest will ripen.

LONDON, *July 22nd*, 1920

The result of the Dyer debates in both Houses of Parliament makes painfully evident the attitude of mind of the ruling classes of this country towards India. It shows that no outrage, however monstrous, committed against us by agents of their Government, can arouse feelings of indignation in the hearts of those from whom our governors are chosen.

The unashamed condonation of brutality expressed in their speeches and echoed in their newspapers is ugly in its frightfulness. The feeling of humiliation about our position under the Anglo-Indian domination had been growing stronger every day for the last fifty years or more; but the one consolation we had was our faith in the love of justice in the English people, whose soul had not been poisoned by that fatal dose of power which could only be available in a Dependency where the manhood of the entire population had been crushed down into helplessness.

Yet the poison has gone further than we expected, and it has attacked the vital organs of the British nation. I feel that our appeal to their higher nature will meet with less and less response every day. I only hope that our countrymen will not lose heart at this, but employ all their energies in the service of their country with a spirit of indomitable courage and determination.

The late events have conclusively proved that our true salvation lies in our own hands; that a nation's greatness can never find its foundation in half-hearted concessions of contemptuous niggardliness.

It is the sign of a feeble character to seek for a short-cut to fulfilment through the favour of those whose interest lies in keeping it barred—the one path to fulfilment is the difficult path of suffering and self-sacrifice. All great boons come to us through the power of the immortal spirit we have within us, and that spirit only proves itself by its defiance of danger and loss.

LONDON, *August 1st*, 1920

We live on the topmost floor of this house far away from the surging life of the town. Only the crest of the swell of the London street-noise reaches me, gently undulating like those clustering tree-tops of Kensington Gardens that I watch from my window. The long and persistent spell of bad weather seems to have exhausted its spite, and the mellow light of the morning sun from behind the fleecy clouds is greeting me like the smile of a child whose eyes are still heavy with sleep. It is nearly seven o'clock, and every one of our party, including Pearson, is fast asleep within shut doors and behind drawn blinds. To-day is our last day in London, and I am not sorry to leave it. I wish it were the day for sailing home, but that day looks hazily distant and my heart aches.

LONDON, *August 4th*, 1920

Owing to a change of plans, we are still detained in London. We hope to leave it the day after to-morrow. Now that people believe that we are away, and since your London weather has ceased to persecute me, these last two days have been very restful for me. I wonder if you know that at the last moment we decided not to start on our tour to Norway, though our tickets were bought. I am sure you are ready to ascribe this to the inconstancy of my mind!

P.S.—I have just written this about Dr. Geddes:—

What so strongly attracted me in Dr. Patrick Geddes when I came to know him in India was not his scientific achievement but, on the contrary, the rare fact of the fullness of his personality rising far above his science. Whatever he has studied and mastered has become vitally one with his humanity. He has the precision of the scientist, and at the same time the vision of the prophet. He has also the power of an artist to make his ideas visible through the language of symbol. His love of man has given him the insight to see the truth of man and imagination to realize in the world not merely the mechanical aspect but also the infinite mystery of life.

PARIS, *August 13th*, 1920

I have come to Paris, not to stay here, but to decide where to go. The sun is shining bright and the spirit of exhilaration is in the atmosphere. Sudhir Rudra received me at the station and made all arrangements for us. Pearson has gone to stay with his mother for some weeks before we start for America. Therefore I am in the hands of Sudhir just at present and he is taking proper care of me. Paris is empty, and there is no chance of our meeting the people whom I should like to meet. Our stay in England has been wasted. Your Parliament debates about Dyerism in the Punjab and other symptoms of an arrogant spirit of contempt and callousness about India have deeply grieved me, and it was with a feeling of relief that I left England.

NEAR PARIS, *August 20th*, 1920

We are in a delightful country, in a delightful place in France, meeting with people who are so human.

I feel clearly that the ultimate reality for man's life is his life in the world of ideas, where he is emancipated from the gravitational pull of the dust and he realizes that he is spirit. We, in India, live in a narrow cage of petty interests; we do not believe that we have wings, for we have lost our sky; we chatter and hop and peck at one another within the small range of our obstructed opportunities. It is difficult to achieve greatness of mind and character where our responsibility is diminutive and fragmentary, where our whole life occupies and affects an extremely limited area.

And yet through the cracks and chinks of our walls we must send out our starved branches to the sunlight and air, and the roots of our life must pierce the upper strata of our soil of desert sands till they reach down to the spring of water which is exhaustless. Our most difficult problem is how to gain our freedom of soul in spite of the cramped condition of our outward circumstances; how to ignore the perpetual insult of our destiny, so as to be able to uphold the dignity of man.

Santiniketan is for this *tapasya* of India. We who have come there often forget the greatness of our mission, mostly because of the obscurity and insignificance with which the humanity of India seems to be obliterated. We have not the proper light and perspective in our surroundings to be able to realize that our soul is great;

and therefore we behave as if we were doomed to be small for all time.

ARDENNES, *August 21st*, 1920

Here we are in a most beautiful part of France. But of what avail is the beauty of Nature when you have lost your trunks which contained all your clothes? I could have been in perfect sympathy with the trees surrounding me if, like them, I were not dependent upon tailors for maintaining self-respect. The most important event for me in this world at present is not what is happening in Poland, or Ireland, or Mesopotamia, but the fact that all the trunks belonging to our party have disappeared from the goods-van in their transit from Paris to this place!

And therefore, though the sea is singing its hymns to the rising and setting sun and to the starlit silence of the night, and though the forest round me is standing tiptoe on the rock, like an ancient Druid, raising its arms to the sky, chanting its incantation of primeval life, we have to hasten back to Paris to be restored to respectability at the hands of tailors and washermen!

I have just received your letter, and for some time I have felt myself held tight in the bosom of our Asram. I cannot tell you how I feel about the prolonged separation from it which is before me; but at the same time I know that unless my relationship with the wide world of humanity grows in truth and love, my relationship with the Asram will not be perfect.

PARIS, *September 7th*, 1920

Your letters always bring the atmosphere of Santiniketan round my mind, with all its colour and sounds and movements; and my love for my boys, like a migratory bird, crosses back over the sea, seeking its own dear nest in the Asram. Your letters are great gifts to me—I have not the power to repay them in kind. For now my mind faces the West, and all that it has to give naturally flows towards it. Therefore, for the time being, my direct communication with you has become thin, like the stream of the Kopai River in the summer. But I know Santiniketan will not bring forth its fullness of flower and fruit if, through me, it does not send its roots into the Western soil. Stung by the insult of cruel injustice, we try to repudiate Europe, but by doing so we insult ourselves. Let us have the dignity not to quarrel or retaliate; not to pay back smallness by being small ourselves. This is the time when we should dedicate all our resources of emotion, thought and character to the service of our country in a positive direction of duty. We are suffering because of our offences against Shivam, against Advaitam. We spend all our energy in quarrelling with the punishment and nothing of it is left for the reparation of wrongs we have done and are doing. When we have performed our part of the duties, we shall have the fullest right and power and time to bring others to book for their transgressions.

Let us forget the Punjab affairs—but never forget that we shall go on deserving such humiliation over and over again until we set our house in order. Do not mind the waves of the sea, but mind the leaks in your vessel. Politics in our country is extremely petty. It has a pair of legs, one of which has shrunk and shrivelled and become paralytic and therefore feebly waits for the other one to drag it on. There is no harmony between the two, and our politics, in its hoppings and totterings and falls, is comic and undignified. The entreaty and anger, which alternately are struggling to find expression in the ludicrously lame member of this tragic partnership, both belong to our abject feebleness. When Non-co-operation comes naturally as our final moral protest against the unnaturalness of our political situation, then it will be glorious, because true; but when it is only another form of begging, then let us reject it.

The establishment of perfect co-operation of life and mind among ourselves must come first, through sacrifice and self-dedication, and then will come in its natural course the non-co-operation. When the fruit completely ripens, it finds its freedom through its own fulfilment of truth.

Our country is crying to her own children for their co-operation in the removal of obstacles in our social life which for centuries have been hampering us in our self-realization. We need co-operation in the sacrifice of love, more than anything else, to prove to our country that she is ours; and then we shall have the moral right to say to others: "We have nothing to do with you in our affairs." And for this, all the moral fervour which the life of Mahatma Gandhi represents, and which he, of all men in the world, can call up, is needed.

That such a precious treasure of power should be put into the mean and frail vessel of our politics, allowing it to sail across endless waves of angry recrimination, is terribly unfortunate for our country, when our mission is to revive the dead with the fire of the soul. The external waste of our resources of life is great owing to external circumstances; but that the waste of our spiritual resources should also be allowed to happen on adventures that are wrong from the point of view of moral truth is heartbreaking. It is criminal to turn moral force into a blind force.

Our time to go to Holland is drawing near. I have numerous invitations from over there to lecture, but I am not yet fully ready. Just now I am busy writing. My subject is the Meeting of the East and West. I hope it will be finished before I leave Paris.

PARIS, *September 12th*, 1920

I had invitations from Germany and decided to go. But travelling from one country to another has become so difficult nowadays that I had to give it up. Specially, going from France to Germany is beset with obstacles. On my way back from Holland, I shall try my best at least to visit Hamburg. Germany needs sympathy, and I hope I shall have the opportunity to go there and offer it to her.

A short time ago I was taken to Rheims and other devastated regions of France in a motor-car. It was a most saddening sight. It will take a tremendous effort and also an immense lapse of time to make this a thing of the past. When the spiritual ideal is lost, when the human relationship is completely broken up, then individuals freed from the creative bond of wholeness find a fearful joy in destruction.

In such catastrophes, one can realize what a stupendous force of annihilation is not only kept in check in our society, but made into multitudinous manifestations of beauty and fruitfulness. Then we know that evils are like meteors, stray fragments, wreckage of a broken-up wholeness, which need the attraction of a great planet of life's ideal to be assimilated into the peace of creation.

Only spiritual ideals have that great power of attraction that can transmute these rebellious fractions into a perfect roundness. The evil forces are literally outlaws. They only need the control and cadence of creative laws to change them into good. Our Shiva[1] is the Lord of terrible spirits, who are spirits of death; and he is also Shivam, the Good. True goodness lies not in the negation of badness, but in the mastery of it. It is the miracle that turns the tumult of chaos into the dance of beauty. True edu-

[1] The God Shiva in Indian mythology is regarded as the Lord of Terrors. But the name "Shivam" indicates beneficence; and thus Shiva is also the God of Goodness. He swallows the deadly poison without harm

cation is that power of miracle, that ideal of creation. Punishments and disciplines imposed from outside are negative. The Teacher is Shiva. He has the divine power of destroying the destructiveness; of sucking out the poison. If France had the Shiva in her heart, she could transform evil into good, she could forgive. And that forgiveness could prove her own immortality, and truly save her from the hurt which was inflicted upon her.

This is difficult; but it is the one way of salvation. Only the creative ideal can completely get over the acts of destruction. It is the spiritual ideal, it is love, it is forgiveness. God is perpetually exercising it, and thus the creation is ever kept sweet.

In the heart of death, life has its ceaseless play of joy.

Do we not know this in our individual life? Have we our own right to exist in this wonderful world? Would we not burn it, destroy it? Has not God's creative power given us our place in His universe? Must we forget that, when we judge and deal with our own fellow-beings?

PARIS, *September 18th*, 1920

I find our countrymen are furiously excited about Non-co-operation. It will grow into something like our Swadeshi movement in Bengal. Such an emotional outbreak should have been taken advantage of in starting independent organizations all over India for serving our country.

Let Mahatma Gandhi be the true leader in this; let him send his call for positive service, ask for homage in sacrifice, which has its end in love and creation. I shall be willing to sit at his feet and do his bidding if he commands me to co-operate with my countrymen in service and love. I refuse to waste my manhood in lighting fires of anger and spreading it from house to house.

It is not that I do not feel anger in my heart for

injustice and insult heaped upon my motherland. But this anger of mine should be turned into the fire of love for lighting the lamp of worship to be dedicated through my country to my God.

It would be an insult to humanity if I use the sacred energy of my moral indignation for the purpose of spreading a blind passion all over my country. It would be like using the fire from the altar of sacrifice for the purpose of incendiarism.

ANTWERP, *October 3rd*, 1920

I have spent about a fortnight in Holland. This fortnight has been most generous in its gifts to me. Of one thing you may be sure, that a communication of heart has been opened up between this little country and Santiniketan; and it remains with us to widen it and make use of it for the interchange of spiritual wealth. Altogether, Europe has come closer to us by this visit of ours. I only wish that all my friends in Santiniketan could realize how true this is and what a wealth it represents. Now I know more clearly than ever before that Santiniketan belongs to the world and we have to be worthy of this great fact It is extremely difficult for us Indians to forget all the irritations that ever keep our consciousness concentrated on our own daily annoyances. But emancipation of consciousness is both the means and end of spiritual life. Therefore Santiniketan must be saved from the whirlwind of our dusty politics.

I am writing this letter from Antwerp, where I came yesterday morning; and I am getting ready to go to Brussels, where I have an invitation. And then I go to Paris.

LONDON, *October 18th*, 1920

Our vision of truth varies according to its perspective. I feel certain that this perspective has become narrow in

India owing to the density of mental atmosphere caused by political unrest. There are politicians who must make hasty decisions and act without delay. It is their function to take short cuts to immediate success and dash through blunders with their lumbering "tanks" of political organizations. But there are needs that belong to all mankind and to all time. Those have to be satisfied through the rise and fall of empires. We all know that there is a vast difference between journalism and literature. Journalism is necessary and there are multitudes of men eager to carry it out. But if it suppresses the light of literature, then it will produce the London fog of November, which substitutes gaslight for the sunlight.

Santiniketan is there for giving expression to the Eternal Man—*asato ma sad gamaya*,[1] the prayer that will ring clearer as the ages roll on, even when the geographical names of all countries are changed and lose their meaning. If I give way to the passion of the moment and the claims of the crowd, then it will be like speculating with my Master's money for a purpose which is not His own.

I know that my countrymen will clamour to borrow from this capital entrusted to me and exploit it for the needs that they believe to be more urgent than anything else. But all the same, you must know that I have to be true to my trust. Santiniketan must treasure in all circumstances that *santi* which is in the bosom of the Infinite. With begging and scrambling we find very little, but with being true to ourselves we find a great deal more than we desire. The best reward that I have gained in my life is through the spontaneous and disinterested expression of truth in me, and never through straining for a result, whatever high-sounding name it may have carried.

---

[1] Lit., "Lead me from Untruth to Truth."

CHAPTER VI

THE journey undertaken to America, described in the letters contained in this chapter, was directly for the purpose of obtaining sympathy and support for the Poet's Visva-bharati ideal. His earlier visits to America in 1913 and 1916 had given him the hope that the young heart of the New World would respond to him more definitely than the peoples of Europe, who were still involved in their national prejudices and their narrow provincial boundaries.

Since the Poet's conception of Visva-bharati lies in the background in all the letters which he wrote to me from America, it may be well as an introduction to this chapter to give his own explanation of his purpose, as he presented it during his lecture tours in India before he started for the West. The following passages from these lectures appear to me to explain the Poet best:—

The age has come when all artificial fences are breaking down. Only that will survive which is basically consistent with the universal; while that which seeks safety in the out-of-the-way hole of the special will perish. The nursery of the infant should be secluded, its cradle safe. But the same seclusion, if continued after the infant has grown up, makes it weak in mind and body.

There was a time when China, Egypt, Greece and Rome had, each of them, to nurture its civilization in comparative seclusion. The greatness of the universal, however, which was more or less in each, grew strong within its protecting sheath of individuality. Now has come the age for co-ordination and co-operation. The seedlings that were reared within their enclosures must now be transplanted into the open fields. They must pass the test of the world-market if their maximum value is to be obtained.

So we must prepare the grand field for the co-ordination of all the cultures of the world, where each will give to and take from the other; where each will have to be studied through the growth of its stages in history. This adjustment of knowledge through comparative study, this progress in intellectual co-operation, is to be the key-note of the coming age. We may hug our holy aloofness from some imagined security of a corner, but the world will prove stronger than our corner, and it is our corner that will have to give way, receding and pressing against its walls till they burst on all sides.

But before we in India are in a position to stand a comparison with the other cultures of the world, or truly to co-operate with them, we must base our structure on a synthesis of all the different cultures we have. When taking our stand at such a centre we turn towards the West, our gaze shall no longer be timid and dazed; our heads shall remain erect, safe from insult. For then we shall be able to take our own views of truth from the standpoint of our own vantage-ground, thus opening out a new vista of thought before a grateful world.

All great countries have their vital centres for intellectual life, where a high standard of learning is maintained, where the minds of the people are naturally attracted to find their genial atmosphere, to prove their worth, to contribute their share to the country's culture, and thus to kindle on some common altar of the land a great sacrificial fire of intellect which may radiate the sacred light in all directions.

Athens was such a centre in Greece, Rome in Italy, and Paris is such to-day in France. Benares has been, and still continues to be, the centre of our Sanskrit culture. But Sanskrit learning does not exhaust all the elements of culture that exist in the present-day India. . . . That is why the inner spirit of India is calling to us to establish in this land great centres, where all her intellectual forces will gather for the purpose of creation, and all her resources of knowledge and thought, Eastern and Western, will unite in perfect harmony. She is seeking for the glorious opportunity to know her own mind and give her mind to the world, to help it in its progress; when she will be released from the chaos of scattered powers and the inertness of borrowed acquisitions.

Let me state clearly that I have no distrust of any culture because of its foreign character. On the contrary, I believe that the shock of such forces is necessary for the vitality of our intellectual nature. It is admitted that much of the spirit of Christianity runs counter, not only to the Classical culture of Europe, but to the European temperament altogether. And yet this alien movement of idea, constantly running against the natural mental current of Europe, has been the most important factor in strengthening and enriching her civilization on account of the very antagonism of its direction. In fact, the European vernaculars first woke up to life and fruitful vigour owing to the impact of this foreign thought-power with all its Oriental forms and feelings. The same thing is happening in India. European culture has come to us, not only with its knowledge, but with its velocity. Though our assimilation of it is imperfect and the consequent aberrations numerous, still it is rousing our intellectual life from its inertia of former habits into growing consciousness by the very contradiction it offers to our mental traditions.

What I object to is the artificial arrangement by which this foreign education tends to occupy all the space of our national mind and thus kills, or hampers, the great opportunity for the creation of a new thought-power by a new combination of truths. It is this which makes me urge that all the elements in our own culture have to be strengthened, not to resist Western culture, but truly to accept and assimilate it; to use it for our food and not as our burden; to get mastery over this culture, and not to live at its outskirts as the hewers of texts and the drawers of book-learning.

Rabindranath Tagore suffered from illness during his visit to America, and this brought with it depression of mind. The response to his appeal for co-operation in his work of international fellowship was not at first as direct and full as he had expected. His longing to go back became at last intense. The letters which he wrote to me during these months were often full of gloom. Those that follow are some of the most important of them dealing with his ideal of a centre of international fellowship at Santiniketan.

NEW YORK, *October 28th*, 1920

Our steamer has arrived in port—too late for us to land to-night. Between one shore and the other there are tossings on the angry waves and menaces of the shrieking winds, but peace comes at the end and shelter when the desolation that divides the world appears unreal and is forgotten. This crossing of the sea has not yet been completed by those who are voyagers from one age to another. Storms have raged and the moaning of the salt sea has haunted their days and nights. But the haven is not very far distant and the new continent of time is ready with its greeting of light and life and its invitation to the unexplored. Already I feel the breath of that future and see birds from the shore bringing songs of hope.

You must know that our Santiniketan belongs to that future. We have not yet reached it. We need stronger faith and clearer vision to direct our course towards its hill of sunlight. There are chains which still keep our boat clinging to the sheltered cove of the past. We must leave it behind. Our loyalty must not be for any land of a limited geography. It should be for the nationality of the common idea, to which are born individuals belonging to various nations, who are carrying their gifts of sacrifice to the one great shrine of Humanity.

NEW YORK, *November 4th*, 1920

There is one thing about which I wish to speak to you. Keep Santiniketan away from the turmoils of politics. I know that the political problem is growing in intensity in India and its encroachment is difficult to resist. But all the same, we must never forget that our mission is not political. Where I have my politics, I do not belong to Santiniketan.

I do not mean to say that there is anything wrong in politics, but only that it is out of harmony with our Asram.

We must clearly realize this fact, that the name of Santiniketan has a meaning for us, and this name will have to be made true. I am anxious and afraid lest the surrounding forces may become too strong for us and we succumb to the onslaught of the present time. Because the time is troubled and the minds of men distracted, all the more must we, through our Asram,* maintain our faith in Shantam, Shivam, Advaitam.

NEW YORK, *November 25th*, 1920

A friend of mine, who is actively interested in my cause, is a Quaker, and he takes me every Sunday morning to the Quakers' meetings. There, in the silence of meditation, I am able to find the eternal perspective of truth, where the vision of outward success dwindles away to its infinitesimal minuteness. What is needed of me is sacrifice. Our payment is for success, but our sacrifice is for truth. If the spirit of sacrifice is pure in quality, then its reward will be more than can be counted and proved, and let my gift to my country and to the world be a life of sacrifice.

But my earnest request to you is to keep your mind high above politics. The problem of this new age is to help to build the world anew. Let us accept this great task. Santiniketan is to make accommodation for the workers from all parts of the world. All other things can wait. We must make room for Man, the guest of this age, and let not the Nation obstruct his path. I am afraid lest the cry of our own sufferings and humiliations should drown the announcement of His coming. For His sake we shall set aside our grievances and shall say: "Whatever may happen to us, let His cause triumph; for the future is His."

NEW YORK, *November 30th*, 1920

I am often reminded of my *Gitanjali* poem in which the woman tells how she found God's sword when she had been seeking for a petal from God's flower-garden. All through my life I have been seeking for such a petal, and I stand puzzled at the sight of the gift waiting for me. This gift has not been my choice, but my God has chosen for me this gift. And now I say to myself that we prove our worthiness for God's gift of responsibility by acceptance of it and not by success or anything else.

The past has been for men, the future is for Man. These *men* are still fighting for the possession of the world: the din and the clash are deafening; the air is obscured with the dust rising from the trampled earth. Standing in the heart of this struggle, we have to build a seat for the one God revealed to all human races. We may be mocked and pushed away by the crowd, but the fact will remain and invisibly grow into truth that we have believed.

I was born a poet, and it is difficult for me to suffer myself to be rudely hustled in my path by busy men who have no leisure for ideas. I am not an athlete. I do not belong to the arena. The stare of the curious crowd scorches my soul. And yet I, of all persons, am called upon to force my way into the thick of the Western public with a mission for which I have never been trained. Truth fashions its own arrows out of reeds that are light and frail.

NEW YORK, *December* 13*th*, 1920

Our Seventh Paus Festival at the Asram is near at hand. I cannot tell you how my heart is thirsting to join you in your festival. I am trying to console myself with the thought that something very big and great is going to be the outcome of the effort I am making. But deep in my heart I know that simplicity of life and endeavour makes for real happiness. When we realize in some measure our ideal of perfection in our work, it matters very little what its dimensions are. Our trust in bigness very often betrays our want of faith in truth. The kingdom of the earth boasts of the magnitude of its possessions, but the Kingdom of Heaven is content with the depth of its self-realization. There are certain institutions which have for their object some external success. But Santiniketan is there for giving us opportunity to realize ourselves in truth. This can never be done through big funds, but through dedication of our life in love.

In this country I live in the dungeon of the Castle of Bigness. My heart is starved. Day and night I dream of Santiniketan, which blossoms like a flower in the atmosphere of the unbounded freedom of simplicity. I know how truly great Santiniketan is, when I view it from this land. Here I feel every day what a terrible nightmare it is for the human soul to bear this burden of the monster Arithmetic. It incessantly drives its victims and yet leads them nowhere. It raises storms of battle which are for sowing broadcast the seeds of future conflict.

The giant reptiles of the primitive earth were proud of their hypertrophied tails, which did not save them from the doom of destruction. I long to leave all this, totally reject this unreality, take the next steamer I can get, and run back to my Santiniketan and serve it with my life and love.

That life which I dedicate to it, if it is true, will make it live. The true wisdom is there, which can spurn the greed for result and is only concerned with the expression of truth. This wisdom found its utterance in India. But there is imminent danger of its being drowned in the flood of noise which the votaries of success are bellowing forth in the prosperous West. My prayer is growing every day more and more intense, to get away from the dark tower of unreality, from this dance of death trampling sweet flowers of life under its tread.

NEW YORK, *December 17th*, 1920

When all my thoughts were furiously revolving, like dead leaves, in a whirlwind of desire for raising funds, a picture came to my hand; it was that of Sujata offering a cup of milk to Buddha. Its message went deep into my heart. It said to me: "The cup of milk comes to you unasked when you have gone through your *tapasya*. It is offered to you with love, and only love can bring its homage to truth."

Then your figure at once came to my mind. The milk has been sent to me through you. It is infinitely more than anything that can come from the cheque-book of the rich. I had become famished in the wilderness of solitude for lack of sympathy and comradeship, when you brought your cup of love to me, which is the true life-giving food freely offered by life. And as the poet Morris says, "Love is enough." That voice of love calls me away from the lure of dollars—the voice that comes to nestle in my heart from across the sea, from the shady avenue of *sal* trees resonant with laughter and songs of simple joy.

The mischief is that ambition does not fully believe in love. It believes in power. It leaves the limpid and singing water of everlasting life for the wine of success. Every day I seem to be growing afraid of the very vision of this success. It had been said in the Upanishad, "Happiness is in greatness." Ambition points out bigness and calls it greatness, and our track is hopelessly lost. When I look at the picture of Buddha, I cry for the great peace of inner fulfilment. My longing grows painfully intense as my mind becomes distracted at the stupendous unmeaningness of monstrosity in things around me. Every morning I sit by my window and say to myself: "I must not bow my head to this ugly idol worshipped by the West with daily human sacrifice." I remember that morning at Shileida when the Vaishnava woman came to me and said: "When are you coming down from your three-storied building to meet your love under the shade of the trees?"

Just now, I am on the top storey of the skyscraper to which the tallest of trees dare not send its whisper; but love silently comes to me saying: "When are you coming down to meet me on the green grass under the rustling leaves, where you have the freedom of the sky and of sunlight and the tender touch of life's simplicity?" I try to say something about money, but it sounds so ludicrous and yet so tragic, that my words grow ashamed of themselves and they stop.

NEW YORK, *December* 19*th*, 1920

When Life began her first experiments, she was mightily proud of the hugeness of her animal specimens. The bigger the bodies were, the more extravagantly large the armour had to be made for their protection. The ludicrous creatures, in order to maintain their balance, had to carry a tail which was absurdly disproportionate to the rest of their bodies. It went on like this till life became a burden to itself and to the exchequer of creation. It was uneconomical, and therefore not only harmful but ungainly. True economy is the principle of beauty in practical arithmetic. Driven to bewilderment, life began to seek for a pause in her insanity of endless multiplication.

All forms of ambitious powers are obsessed by this delirium of multiplication. All its steps are steps towards augmentation and not completeness. But ambitions, that rely solely upon the suggestion of their tails and armour, are condemned to carry their own obstruction till they have to stop.

In its early history, Life, after its orgies of megalomania, had at last to think of disarmament. But how did she effect it? By boldly relinquishing the ambition to produce bigness—and man was born helplessly naked and small. All of a sudden he was disinherited of the enormity of flesh, when apparently he was most in need of it. But this prodigious loss gained for him his freedom and victory.

Then began the reign of Mind. It brought its predecessor of gigantic bulk under subjection. But, as often happens, the master became the parasite of the slave, and mind also tried to achieve greatness by the bigness of materials. The dynasty of mind followed the dynasty of flesh, but employed this flesh as its prime minister.

Our history is waiting for the dynasty of Spirit. The human succeeded the brutal; and now comes the turn of the Divine.

In our mythology we have often heard of a man taking the side of the Gods and saving Paradise from the dominion of Giants. But in our history we often notice man holding alliance with Giants and trying to defeat the Gods. His guns and ships of huge power and proportion are turned out from the arsenal of the Giant. In the fight of bigness against goodness, man has joined the former, counting the coins of his reward in number and not in quality—in lead and not in gold.

Those who are in possession of material resources have become slaves of their own instruments. Fortunately for us, in India, these resources are beyond all immediate possibility of realization. We are disarmed, and therefore we have no option but to seek for other and higher sources of power. The men who believe in the reality of brute force have made enormous sacrifices in order to maintain it. Let us, in India, have faith in the moral power in man and be ready to sacrifice for it all we have. Let us do our best to prove that Man has not been the greatest mistake in Creation. Let it not be said that, for the sake of peace and happiness in the world, the physical brutes were preferable to the intellectual brutes who boast of their factory-made teeth and nails and poison fangs.

New York, *December 20th*, 1920

In every age and in every country facts are given to us in order that we may provide with them some special expression of Truth. Facts are like atoms in gases: they fight with, or else fly away from, one another. But when they are united into a drop of dew they attain beauty and reality. Man must have that creative magic to bring the facts of his time into some unity of creation. In Christ and in Buddha this creative ideal tried to unite men who were divided because of their formalism in religious faith.

Formalism in religion is like nationalism in politics: it breeds sectarian arrogance, mutual misunderstanding and a spirit of persecution. Our Indian mediæval saints, through their light of love and inner perception of truth, could realize the spiritual unity of man. For them, the innumerable barriers of formalism had no existence. Therefore the mutually antagonistic creeds of Hindus and Muhammadans, irreconcilable as they seemed, did not baffle them. Our faith in truth has its trial in the apparent difficulty of its realization.

The most important of all facts in the present age is that the East and West have met. So long as it remains a mere fact, it will give rise to interminable conflicts; it will even hurt man's soul. It is the mission of all men of faith to raise this fact into truth. The worldly-wise will shake their heads and say it is not possible—that there is a radical difference between the East and the West and that only physical power will have its sway in their relationship.

But physical power is not creative. Whatever laws and organizations it may produce, it will never satisfy spiritual humanity. Ram Mohun Roy was the first great man in our age who had the profound faith and large vision to feel in his heart the unity of soul between the East and West. I follow him, though he is practically rejected by my countrymen.

I only wish you had been with me in Europe! You would know at once what was the purpose of the modern age; what is the cry of man, which the politicians never hear. There were politicians in the courts of the Moghul Emperors. They have left nothing behind them but ruins. But Kabir and Nanak! They have bequeathed to us their imperishable faith in the unity of man through God's love.

NEW YORK, *December 21st*, 1920

All about me is a desert of crowds, a monotony of multitude. Man is drowned in his own deluge of desultoriness. It is an unceasing struggle in me to have to pass through this—especially when I carry in myself such a heavy load of helplessness. Every moment I am made conscious of it, and I am tired. When we have the banner of an idea to carry against obstacles of indifference, the burden of our personal self should be extremely light. But I am so awkwardly cumbersome with my ineptitude.

I remember, when I was young, how a blind old beggar used to come to our door every morning led by a boy. It was a tragic sight; the blindness of the old man robbed the boy of his freedom. The boy looked so wistful and eager for release. Our incapacity is a fetter with which we tie others to our limitations. Consciousness of this, every day adds to my feeling of weariness. But this depression of spirit is likely to do me a service. It has led me to the brink of a discovery that a great measure of one's impotence is *maya*.

Latterly I have been constantly giving myself a shaking, trying to arouse myself from this stupor of self-delusion. During the greater part of my life my mind has been made accustomed to travel the inner paths of dreams, till it has lost all confidence in its power to thread its way through the zigzags of the outer world. In fact, its attention has never been trained to accept the miscellaneous responsibilities of the clamorous surface life of society. Therefore the West is not my world.

And yet I have received the gift of love from the West,

and my heart acknowledges her claims to my service and I must unreservedly offer myself to her before I die. I do not belong to the present age, the age of conflicting politics. Nevertheless I cannot repudiate the age which has given me birth. I suffer and struggle. I crave for freedom and yet am held back. I must share the life of the present world, though I do not believe in its cry. I sit at its table, and while it fills its cup with wine to slake its unnatural thirst, I try to listen, through the noisy carousal, to the murmur of the stream carrying its limpid waters to the sea.

NEW YORK, *December 22nd*, 1920

To-day is the seventh of Paus. I wish it were allowed to me to stand among you and mingle my voice with yours in uttering our prayer. It is real starvation of my heart to be deprived of this great privilege. To-day I realize more than ever before that nothing can be truer for me than to be with my dear children and friends, this beautiful sunny morning of December, and bow my head to my Father and dedicate my service to Him. By that dedication our works become great, and not by extension of external resources.

Oh, how simple is truth and how full of light and happiness! Not to be distracted by the curiosity of crowds, only to be rewarded by the approval of Him who knows our heart, in the fulfilment of our endeavour. I only hope that what I am doing here is in response to the call of the Shantam, that my lonely celebration of seventh Paus in this hotel room finds its harmony with your festival. Let our faith in the real be not overcome by the lure of the unreal. Let come to us what is good and not what we desire. Let us bow our heads to the Good, to the supreme Good.[1]

---

[1] These sentences are a free translation of the prayer repeated together in the *mandir* (or chapel) at Santiniketan.

I have often felt the desire that you were with me in my adventure. And yet I am deeply thankful that you could remain at the Asram while I was away. For you understand me with the understanding of love, and therefore through you I seem to dwell in Santiniketan. I know that I am in your mind to-day and you know that my heart is with you. Is it not a great good fortune that there is a spot in this world where all that is best in us can meet in truth and love? Can anything be greater than that? Please give my blessings to all my boys and girls, and my greetings of love to my friends.

NEAR NEW YORK, *December 25th*, 1920

To-day is Christmas Day. We are about forty-five guests gathered in this inn from different parts of the United States. It is a beautiful house, nestling in the heart of a wooded hill, with an invitation floating in the air of a brook broadening into a lake in the valley. It is a glorious morning, full of peace and sunlight, of the silence of the leafless forest untouched by bird songs or humming of bees.

But where is the spirit of Christmas in human hearts? The men and women are feeding themselves with extra dishes and laughing extra loud. But there is not the least touch of the eternal in the heart of their merriment, no luminous serenity of joy, no depth of devotion. How immensely different from the religious festivals of our country! These Western people have made their money but killed their poetry of life. Here life is like a river, that has heaped up gravel and sand and choked the perennial current of water that flows from an eternal source on the snowy height of an ancient hill. I have learnt since I came here to prize more than ever the infinite worth of the frugal life and simple faith. These Western people believe in their wealth, which can only multiply itself and attain nothing.

How to convince them of the utter vanity of their pursuits! They do not have the time to realize that they are not happy. They try to smother their leisure with rubbish of dissipation, lest they discover that they are the unhappiest of mortals. They deceive their souls with counterfeits, and then, in order to hide that fact from themselves, they artificially keep up the value of those false coins by an unceasing series of self-deceptions.

My heart feels like a wild-duck from the Himalayan lake lost in the endless desert of Sahara, where sands glitter with a fatal brilliance but the soul withers for want of the life-giving spring of water.

NEW YORK, *January 8th*, 1921

There are a large number of ideas about which we do not even know that they are inaccessible to us, only because we have grown too familiar with their names.

Such is our idea of God. We do not have to realize it in order to be made aware of it. This is why it requires a great deal of spiritual sensitiveness to be able to feel the life-throb of God's reality behind the vulgar callosity of words. Things that are small naturally come to their limits for us, when they are familiar. But the truth which is great should reveal its infinity all the more vastly when it is near to us. Unfortunately, words that represent truth have not the same immensity of life as truth itself. Therefore the words (and with them our attention and interest) become inert by constant handling, obscuring our faith underneath them without our being conscious of that tragic fact.

This is the reason why men who are obviously religious are frequently more irreligious, in reality, than those who openly ignore religion. Preachers and ministers of religion have made it their business to deal with God at every moment. They cannot afford to wait until they come in touch with Him. They dare not acknowledge the fact that they have not done so. Therefore they have to strain their minds into a constant attitude of God-Knowingness. They have to delude themselves, in order to fulfil the expectations of others, or what they consider to be their duty.

And yet the consciousness of God, like that of all other ideas, comes to us only with intense moments of illumination, of inspiration. If we do not have the patience to wait for it, we only choke the path of inspiration with the *débris* of our conscious efforts. Those who make it their business to preach God, preach creeds. They lose their sense of distinction between these two. Therefore their religion does not bring peace into this world, but conflict. They do not hesitate to make use even of their religion for the propaganda of national self-seeking and boastfulness.

You may wonder, in your mind, as to the reason of my bringing up this topic in my present letter. It is in connection with the same endless conflict within me between the poet and the preacher, one of whom depends for his mission upon inspiration and the other upon conscious endeavour. Straining of consciousness leads to insensitiveness, of which I am more afraid than anything else. The preacher is the professional dealer in particular ideas. His customers come at all hours of the day and put questions to him. The answers, which he gets into the habit of producing, gradually lose their living quality, and his faith in his ideas runs the risk of being smothered under the deadness of his words. I believe that such a tragedy is more common than people suspect, especially with those who are good and therefore are ever ready to sign their cheque of benefit for others without waiting to see if the cash has had time to accumulate in the bank.

This makes me think that it is safe to be nothing

better than a mere poet. For poets have to be true to their best moments and not to other peoples' requirements.

NEW YORK, *January 14th*, 1921

Even when I was very young my mind ever sought for all experiences in an environment of completeness. That is to say, fact indicated some truth to me, even though I did not clearly understand it. That is why my mind was constantly struck with things that in themselves were commonplace.

When I watched, from over the wall of the terrace of the inner apartments of our Jorashanko house, the coconut-trees and the tank surrounded by the huts of the milk vendors, they came before me with a more-than-themness that could not be exhausted. That faculty —though subsequently mingled with reasoning and self-analysis—has still continued in my life. It is the sense and craving for wholeness. Constantly it has been the cause of my separation from others and also their misunderstanding of my motives.

Swadeshi, Swarajism, ordinarily produce intense excitement in the minds of my countrymen, because they carry in them some fervour of passion generated by the exclusiveness of their range. It cannot be said that I am untouched by this heat and movement. But somehow, by my temperament as a poet, I am incapable of accepting these objects as final. They claim from us a great deal more than is their due. After a certain point is reached, I find myself obliged to separate myself from my own people, with whom I have been working, and my soul cries out: "The complete man must never be sacrificed to the patriotic man, or even to the merely moral man."

To me humanity is rich and large and many-sided. Therefore I feel deeply hurt when I find that, for some material gain, man's personality is mutilated in the Western world and he is reduced to a machine.

The same process of repression and curtailment of humanity is often advocated in our country under the name of patriotism. Such deliberate impoverishment of our nature seems to me a crime. It is a cultivation of callousness, which is a form of sacrilege. For God's purpose is to lead man into perfection of growth, which is the attainment of a unity comprehending an immense manifoldness. But when I find man, for some purpose of his own, imposing upon his society a mutilation of mind, a niggardliness of culture, a puritanism which is spiritual penury, it makes me inexpressibly sad.

I have been reading a book by a Frenchman on Japan. The sensitiveness to the ideal of beauty, which has been made universal in Japan, is not only the source of her strength, but of her heroic spirit of renunciation. For true renunciation blossoms on the vigorous soil of beauty and joy—the soil which supplies positive food to our souls.

But the negative process of making the soil poor produces a ghastly form of renunciation which belongs to the nihilism of life. An emancipation of human nature has already been going on for a long time in India. Let us not add to it by creating a mania for self-immolation. Our life to-day needs more colour, more expansion, more nourishment, for all the variety of its famished functions. Whatever may be the case in other countries, we need in India more fullness of life, and not asceticism.

Deadness of life, in all forms, gives rise to impurities, by enfeebling our reason, narrowing our vision, creating fanaticism, owing to our will-power being forced into abnormal channels. Life carries its own purification when its sap finds the passage unbarred through all ramifications.

NEW YORK, *January 23rd*, 1921

I have just come back from Greenwich, a suburban part of New York, where last night I had a reception and a speech and a dinner and a discussion, till I felt empty, like a burst balloon with no gas left in it!

At the far-distant end of the wilderness of such trials as this what do I see? But what matters it? Results of our efforts delude us by appearing as final. They raise expectation of fulfilment and draw us on. But they are not final. They are roadside inns where we change our horses for a farther journey. An ideal is different. It carries its own progress within itself. Each stage is not a mere approach to the goal, but carries with it its own meaning and purpose.

Trees proceed on their upward career, not along a railway track constructed by engineers. We, who have been dreamers, should never employ coolies to build railway lines of social service. We must solely deal with living ideas, and have faith in life. Otherwise we are punished, not necessarily with bankruptcy, but with success—behind which sits the Mephistopheles of worldliness, chuckling at the sight of an idealist dragged through the dust by the chariot of the prosperous.

What has made us love Santiniketan so deeply is the ideal of perfection, which we have tasted all through its growth. It has not been made by money, but by our love, our life. With it we need not strain for any result; it is fulfilment itself—the life which forms round it, the service which we daily render it. Now I realize, more than ever before, how precious and how beautiful is the simplicity of our Asram, which can reveal itself all the more luminously because of its background of material poverty and want.

New York, *February 2nd*, 1921

After a break of three weeks and a sultriness of weary waiting, your letters have come in a downpour; and I cannot possibly tell you how refreshing they are! I seem to be travelling across a desert, and your letters are like weekly provisions dropped by some air-service from cloud-land. They are expected; and yet they have the element of surprise. I hungrily attack them and fall upon extra portions supplied from your letters written to others.

Your letters are delightful, because you have your interest in details that are generally overlooked. The world is made beautiful by the unimportant things. They furnish this great world-picture with all its modulations of shades and tints. The important things are like the sunshine. They come from a great source. But the unimportant compose the atmosphere of our life. They scatter the sun's rays, break the atmosphere into colours, and coax it into tenderness.

You have asked for my permission to abolish the matriculation class from our school. Let it go. I have no tenderness for it. In our classical literature it was the strict rule to give all dramas a happy ending. Our matriculation class has ever been the fifth act in our Asram, ending in a tragedy. Let us drop the scene, before that disaster gathers its forces!

I am enclosing with this a translation, which runs thus:—

WOMAN

The fight is ended.
Shrill cries of loss trouble the air,
The gains, soiled and shattered, are a burden too heavy
to carry home.

Come, woman, bring thy breath of life.
Close all cracks with kisses of tender green,
  Nurse the trampled dust into fruitfulness.

The morning wears on;
The stranger sits homeless by the roadside, playing on his reed.
Come, woman, bring thy magic of love!
Make infinite the corner between walls,
There to build a world for him,—
Thine eyes its stars, thy voice its music.

The gate-door creaks in the wind.
The time is for leave-taking at the day's end.
Come woman, bring thy tears!
Let thy tremulous touch call out its last lyric
  From the moment of parting.
Let the shadow of thy sad gaze
  Haunt the road across the hills.

The night deepens;
The house is empty; its loneliness aches with silence.
Come, woman, bring thy lamp of vigil!
Enter thy secret chamber of sorrow.
Make the dark hours quiver with the agony of thy prayer,
Till the day dawns in the East.

NEW YORK, *February 5th*, 1921

Civilization in the West is a magnifying glass. It makes the most ordinary things hugely big. Its buildings, business, amusements, are exaggerations. The spirit of the West loves its high-heeled boots, whose heels are much bigger than itself.

Since I came to this continent my arithmetic has

become absurdly bloated. It refuses to be compressed within decent limits. But I can assure you that to carry such a burden even in my imagination is wearisome.

Yesterday some Santiniketan photographs came by chance into my hands. I felt as if I was suddenly wakened up from a Brobdingnagian nightmare. I say to myself, This is our Santiniketan. It is ours, because it is not manufactured by a machine. Truth is beautiful—like woman in our own country. She never strains to add to her inches by carrying extravagances under her feet. Happiness is not in success, not in bigness, but in truth.

What makes me feel so sad, in this country, is the fact that people here do not know that they are not happy. They are proud, like the sandy desert, which is proud of its glitter. This Sahara is mightily big; but my mind turns its back upon it, and sings:—

I will arise and go now, and go to Innisfree,
And a small cabin build there, of clay and wattles made;
Nine bean rows will I have there, a hive for the honey-bee,
And live alone in the bee-loud glade.

In the modern age, with all its facilities of communication, the access to Innisfree has become most difficult. Central Africa opens its secret to the inquisitive man, and also the North and South Pole—but the road to Innisfree lies in an eternal mystery.

Yet I belong to that "Isle of Innisfree": its true name is Santiniketan. But when I leave it, and cross over to the western shore, I feel occasionally frightened lest I should lose my path back to it.

Oh! but how sweet is our *Sal* avenue, the breath of

Rabindranath Tagore

From the dry point by Mukul Dey

autumn in our *Shiuli* groves, the rainy evening resonant with music in Dinu's absurd little room!

And I shall have some peace there, for peace comes dropping slow,
Dropping from the veils of the morning to where the cricket sings;
There midnight's all a glimmer and noon a purple glow,
And evening full of the linnet's wings.

CHAPTER VII

DURING the months of February and March 1921 the Non-co-operation movement reached its height in India. The appeal made to boycott the Government Schools and Colleges stirred the hearts of the students of Calcutta and some thousands of them came out. The atmosphere was electrical and the spirit of sacrifice was in the very air we breathed. My letters to the Poet were full of these things, and I myself was carried away in the enthusiasm of the moment. It is necessary to understand that the letters which the Poet wrote to me at this time were, in part at least, his own reaction to this news which reached him, week by week, from me. Gradually, as his health improved, his stay in America became brighter, and he wrote more cheerfully. He was specially delighted with his first visit to the Southern States, and deeply appreciated the warmth of heart he found among every class of people in those regions. With this very brief note of explanation, the letters that follow tell their own story and are easily intelligible.

On the voyage to Europe the Poet wrote, day after day, a separate letter to me. He did the same on his later journey from Europe to India and with some amusement gave me the whole series from his own letter-case on arrival at Santiniketan. This will account for the different letters written on board ship which are reproduced in this volume.

NEW YORK, *February 8th*, 1921

I have just read a letter published in *Prabasi* by one who is at the Asram, and it has deeply hurt me. This is the ugliest side of patriotism. For in small minds, patriotism dissociates itself from the higher ideal of humanity. It becomes the magnification of self, on a stupendous scale—magnifying our vulgarity, cruelty, greed; dethroning God, to put up this bloated self in its place.

The whole world is suffering from this cult of Devil-worship in the present age, and I cannot tell you how deeply I am suffering, being surrounded in this country by endless ceremonials of this hideously profane cult. Everywhere there is an antipathy against Asia vented by a widespread campaign of calumny. Negroes are burnt alive, sometimes merely because they tried to exercise their right to vote, given to them by law. Germans are reviled. Conditions in Russia are deliberately misrepresented. They are furiously busy building their towers of political civilization upon the quagmire of mob psychology, spreading over it a crust of deliberate lies. They have to subsist upon a continual supply of hatred, contempt, jealousy, and lies and lies!

I am afraid I shall be rejected by my own people when I go back to India. My solitary cell is awaiting me in my motherland. In their present state of mind, my countrymen will have no patience with me, who believe God to be higher than my country.

I know such spiritual faith may not lead us to political success, but I say to myself, as India has ever said: "Even then—what?"

The more I live in this country the more I understand the true meaning of emancipation.

It is for India to keep her breast supplied with the *Amrita*[1] of wisdom, with which to feed the new-born age and nourish it into a mighty future.

The ideas to which politicians still cling belong to a past that is doomed. It is a wreck rushing towards annihilation. The West is beginning to have doubts about its shelter, but its habit of mind is preventing it from leaving the old shelter for a new one. But we unfortunate creatures are getting ready to jump into the stream and swim across to the sinking ship and fight for our place in its corner. Yet I know that our huts are safer than that doomed and drifting monster.

I long to live in the heart of Peace. I have done my work, and I hope that my Master will grant me leave to sit by Him, not to talk, but to listen to His own great silence.

HOUSTON, TEXAS, *February* 23*rd*, 1921

Tied to the chariot-wheel of Karma we flit from one birth to another. What that means to the individual soul I have been made to realize in these last few days. It is my tyrant Karma which is dragging me from one hotel to another. Between my two hotel incarnations I usually have my sleep in a Pullman car, the very name of which suggests the agency of death. I am ever dreaming of the day when I shall attain my Nirvana, freed from this chain of hotel lives, and reach utter peace in Uttarayana.[2]

I have not written to you for some time. For I am tired to the profound depth of my being.

Yet, since coming to Texas, I have felt as it were a sudden coming of Spring into my life through a breach in the ice castle of Winter. It has come to me like a revelation that all these days my soul had been thirsting for the draught of sunshine poured from the beaker of

[1] *Amrita* is the divine nectar which gives immortal life.

[2] The Poet's cottage at Santiniketan.

infinite space. The sky has embraced me, and the warmth of its caress thrills me with joy.

CHICAGO, *February 24th*, 1921

We have engaged our passage in a Dutch steamer, which will sail from New York on the 19th of March. My days in this country have not given me much pleasure—the simple course would have been for me to go straight back home.

Why did I not do so? No fool can say why he has been foolish. I have often dreamed of the time when my wayward youth took me to the loneliness of the sandbanks of the Padma, wandering in the neighbourhood of the wild-ducks under the gaze of the evening star. Certainly, that was not the life of the sane, but it fitted me like a fool's cap lined with dreams.

The fool who is content to do nothing whatever is at any rate free from care; but the one who tries in vain to change the face of the world knows no peace. I long to go back to my ducks, and yet I madly whirl round these manufacturing towns like a breath of the wild south breeze stirring the leaves of the documents of an attorney's office. Does it not know that these leaves do not shelter the flowers that wait for its whisper of love? Why should I be anything else but a poet? Was I not born a music-maker?

CHICAGO, *February 26th*, 1921

I have often wondered in my mind whether my path is the path of the good. When I came to this world I had nothing but a reed given to me, which was to find its only value in producing music. I left my school, I neglected my work, but I had my reed and I played on it "in mere idle sport." All along I had my one playmate, who also in His play produced music, among leaves, in rushing water, in silence of stars, in tears and laughter rippling into lights and shadows in the stream of human life. While my companion was this eternal Piper, this Spirit of play, I was nearest to the heart of the world. I knew its mother-tongue, and what I sang was caught up by the chorus of the wind and water and the dance-master of life.

But now came the schoolmaster in the midst of my dream-world, and I was foolish enough to accept his guidance. I laid aside my reed, I left my playground, where the Infinite Child is spending his eternity "in mere idle sport." In a moment I became old and carried the burden of wisdom on my back, hawking truths from door to door.

Why have I been made to carry this burden, I ask myself over and over again, shouting myself hoarse in this noisy world where everybody is crying up his own wares? Pushing the wheelbarrows of propaganda from continent to continent—is this going to be the climax of a poet's life? It seems to me like an evil dream, from which I occasionally wake up in the dead of night and grope about in the bed asking myself in consternation: "Where is my music?"

It is lost, but I had no right to lose it, for I did not earn it with the sweat of my brow; it was a gift to me, which I could deserve if I knew how to love it. You know I have said somewhere that "God praises me when I do good; but God loves me when I sing." Praise is reward; it can be measured against the work you render; but love is above all rewards; it is measureless.

The poet who is true to his mission reaps his harvest of love; but the poet who strays into the path of the good is dismissed with applause. So I founded my International University—a great work! But I lose my little song—which loss can never be made up to me. How I wish I could find my reed again and be contemptuously ignored by the busy and the wise as a hopeless ne'er-do-well!

When I know for certain that I shall never be able to go back to that sweet obscurity which is the birthplace of flowers and songs, I feel home-sick. It is a world which is so near and yet so far away; so easy of access and yet so immensely difficult. Happiness we go on missing in our life, because it is so simple.

CHICAGO, *March 2nd*, 1921

Your last letter gives wonderful news about our students in Calcutta.[1] I hope that this spirit of sacrifice and willingness to suffer will grow in strength; for to achieve this is an end in itself. This is the true freedom! Nothing is of higher value—be it national wealth or independence—than disinterested faith in ideals, in the moral greatness of man.

The West has its unshakable faith in material strength and prosperity; and therefore, however loud grows the cry for peace and disarmament, its ferocity growls louder, gnashing its teeth and lashing its tail in impatience. It is like a fish, hurt by the pressure of the flood, planning to fly in the air. Certainly the idea is brilliant, but it is not possible for a fish to realize. We, in India, have to show the world what is that truth which not only makes disarmament possible but turns it into strength.

The truth that moral force is a higher power than brute force will be proved by the people who are unarmed. Life, in its higher development, has thrown off its tremendous burden of armour and a prodigious quantity of flesh, till man has become the conqueror of the brute world. The day is sure to come when the frail man of spirit, completely unhampered by air-fleets and dreadnoughts, will prove that the meek are to inherit the earth.

It is in the fitness of things that Mahatma Gandhi, frail in body and devoid of all material resources, should

[1] Referring to the boycott of schools and colleges by thousands of students.

call up the immense power of the meek that has been waiting in the heart of the destitute and insulted humanity of India. The destiny of India has chosen for its ally the power of soul, and not that of muscle. And she is to raise the history of man from the muddy level of physical conflict to the higher moral altitude.

What is Swaraj! It is *maya*; it is like a mist that will vanish, leaving no stain on the radiance of the Eternal. However we may delude ourselves with the phrases learnt from the West, Swaraj is not our objective. Our fight is a spiritual fight—it is for Man. We are to emancipate Man from the meshes that he himself has woven round him—these organizations of national egoism. The butterfly will have to be persuaded that the freedom of the sky is of higher value than the shelter of the cocoon. If we can defy the strong, the armed, the wealthy—revealing to the world the power of the immortal spirit—the whole castle of the Giant Flesh will vanish in the void. And then Man will find his Swaraj.

We, the famished ragged ragamuffins of the East, are to win freedom for all humanity. We have no word for "Nation" in our language. When we borrow this word from other people, it never fits us. For we are to make our league with *Narayan*,[1] and our triumph will not give us anything but victory itself: victory for God's world. I have seen the West; I covet not the unholy feast in which she revels every moment, growing more and more bloated and red and dangerously delirious. Not for us is this mad orgy of midnight, with lighted torches, but awakenment in the serene light of the morning.

CHICAGO, *March 5th*, 1921

Lately I have been receiving more and more news and newspaper cuttings from India, giving rise in my mind to

[1] The godlike element in man

a painful struggle that presages a period of suffering which is waiting for me. I am striving with all my power to tune my mood of mind to be in accord with the great feeling of excitement sweeping across my country. But, deep in my being, why is there this spirit of resistance maintaining its place in spite of my strong desire to remove it? I fail to find a clear answer; and through my gloom of dejection breaks out a smile and a voice saying: "Your place is on 'the sea-shore of worlds,' with children; there is your peace, and I am with you there."

This is why lately I have been playing with inventing new metres. These are merest nothings that are content to be borne away by the current of time, dancing in the sun and laughing as they disappear. But while I play, the whole creation is amused, for are not flowers and leaves never-ending experiments in metres? Is not my God an eternal waster of time? He flings stars and planets in the whirlwind of changes, he floats paper-boats of ages, filled with his fancies, on the rushing stream of appearance. When I tease him and beg him to allow me to remain his little follower and accept a few trifles of mine as the cargo of his play-boat, he smiles and I trot behind him catching the hem of his robe.

But where am I among the crowd, pushed from behind, pressed from all sides? And what is this noise about me? If it is a song, then my own *sitar* can catch the tune and I can join in the chorus; for I am a singer. But if it is a shout, then my voice is wrecked, and I am lost in bewilderment. I have been trying all these days to find in it a melody, straining my ear, but the idea of non-co-operation, with its mighty volume of sound, does not sing to me; its congregated menace of negation shouts. And I say to myself: "If you cannot keep step with your countrymen at this great crisis of their history, never say that you are right and the rest of them wrong; only, give up your rôle as a soldier, go back to your corner as a poet, be ready to accept popular derision and disgrace."

R——, in support of the present movement, has often said to me that passion for rejection is a stronger power in the beginning than the acceptance of an ideal. Though I know this to be a fact, I cannot take it as a truth. We must choose our allies once for all; for they stick to us even when we might be glad to be rid of them. If we once claim strength from intoxication, then in the time of reaction our normal strength is bankrupt, and we go back again and again to the demon that lends us resources in a vessel whose bottom it takes away.

Brahma-vidya, the cult of Brahma, the Infinite Being, has for its object *mukti*, emancipation; while Buddhism has *nirvana*, extinction. It may be argued that both have the same ideas in different names. But names represent attitudes of mind and emphasize particular aspects of truth. *Mukti* draws our attention to the positive, and *nirvana* to the negative side of truth. Buddha kept silence through his teachings about the truth of the *Om*, the Everlasting Yes, his implication being that by the negative path, destroying the self, we naturally reach that truth. Therefore he emphasized the fact of *dukkha*, misery, which had to be avoided. But *Brahma-vidya* emphasized the fact of *ananda*, joy, which had to be attained. The latter cult also needs for its fulfilment the discipline of self-abnegation; yet it holds before its view the idea of Brahma, not only at the end, but all through the process of realization.

Therefore the idea of life's training was different in the Vedic period from that of the Buddhistic. In the former it was the purification of life's joy; in the latter it was the eradication of it. The abnormal type of asceticism, to which Buddhism gave rise in India, revelled in celibacy and mutilation of life in all different forms. The forest life of the Brahman was not antagonistic to the social life of man, but harmonious with it. It was like our musical instrument, the *tambura*, whose duty is to supply the fundamental notes to the music to save it from straying into discordance. It believed in the music of the soul, and its own simplicity was not to kill it, but to guide it.

The idea of non-co-operation is political asceticism. Our students are bringing their offering of sacrifices to what? Not to a fuller education, but to non-education. It has at its back a fierce joy of annihilation, which at its best is asceticism, and at its worst that orgy of frightfulness in which human nature, losing faith in the basic reality of normal life, finds a disinterested delight in an unmeaning devastation, as has been shown in the late war and on other occasions which came nearer to us. "No," in its passive moral form, is asceticism, and in its active moral form violence. The desert is as much a form of *himsa*, violence, as is the raging sea in storm; they are both against life.

I remember the day, during the Swadeshi movement in Bengal, when a crowd of young students came to see me in the first floor of our Vichitra[1] house. They said to me that if I would order them to leave their schools and colleges they would instantly obey. I was emphatic in my refusal to do so, and they went away angry, doubting the sincerity of my love for my motherland. And yet long before this popular ebullition of excitement, I myself had given a thousand rupees, when I had not five rupees to call my own, to open a Swadeshi store and courted banter and bankruptcy.

The reason of my refusal to advise those students to leave their schools was because the anarchy of mere

[1] The Poet's hall of music in Calcutta.

emptiness never tempts me, even when it is resorted to as a temporary measure. I am frightened at an abstraction which is ready to ignore living reality. These students were no mere phantoms to me. Their life was a great fact to them and to the All. I could not lightly take upon myself the tremendous responsibility of a mere negative programme for them which would uproot their life from its soil, however thin and poor that soil might be. The great injury and injustice which had been done to those boys, who were tempted away from their career before any real provision was made, could never be made good to them. Of course, that is nothing from the point of view of an abstraction, which can ignore the infinite value even of the smallest fraction of reality. I wish I were the little creature Jack, whose one mission is to kill the Giant Abstraction, which is claiming the sacrifice of individuals all over the world under highly painted masks of delusion.

I say again and again that I am a poet; that I am not a fighter by nature. I would give everything to be one with my surroundings.

I love my fellow-beings and prize their love. Yet I have been chosen by destiny to ply my boat at that spot where the current is against me. What irony of fate is this, that I should be preaching co-operation of cultures between East and West on this side of the sea just at the moment when the doctrine of non-co-operation is preached on the other side!

You know that I do not believe in the material civilization of the West, just as I do not believe the physical body to be the highest truth in man. But I believe still less in the destruction of the physical body, and the ignoring of the material necessities of life. What is needed is the establishment of harmony between the physical and spiritual nature of man, the maintaining of balance between the foundation and superstructure. I believe in the true meeting of East and West. Love is the ultimate truth of soul. We should do all we can not to outrage that truth, but to carry its banner against all opposition. The idea of non-co-operation unnecessarily hurts that truth. It is not our hearth-fire, but the fire that burns out our hearth and home.

NEW YORK, *March 13th*, 1921

Things that are stationary have no responsibility and need no law. For death, even the tombstone is a useless luxury. But for a world, which is an ever-moving multitude advancing towards an idea, all its laws must have one principle of harmony. This is the law of creation.

Man became great when he found out this law for himself, the law of co-operation. It helped him to move together, to utilize the rhythm and impetus of the world march. He at once felt that this moving together was not mechanical, not an external regulation for the sake of some convenience. It was what the metre is in poetry—not a mere system of enclosure for keeping ideas from running away in disorder, but for vitalizing them, making them indivisible in a unity of creation.

So far this idea of co-operation has developed itself into individual communities, within the boundaries of which peace has been maintained and varied wealth of life produced. But outside these boundaries the law of co-operation has not been realized. Consequently the great world of man is suffering from ceaseless discordance. We are beginning to discover that our problem is world-wide, and no one people of the earth can work out its salvation by detaching itself from others. Either we shall be saved together or drawn together into destruction.

This truth has ever been recognized by all the great personalities of the world. They had in themselves the perfect consciousness of the undivided spirit of man. Their teachings were against tribal exclusiveness, and thus we find that Buddha's India transcended geographical India and Christ's religion broke through the bonds of Judaism.

To-day, at this critical moment of the world's history, cannot India rise above her limitations and offer the great ideal to the world that will work towards harmony and co-operation between the different peoples of the earth? Men of feeble faith will say that India requires to be strong and rich before she can raise her voice for the sake of the whole world. But I refuse to believe it. That the measure of man's greatness is in his material resources is a gigantic illusion casting its shadow over the present-day world—it is an insult to man. It lies in the power of the materially weak to save the world from this illusion; and India, in spite of her penury and humiliation, can afford to come to the rescue of humanity.

The freedom of unrestrained egoism in the individual is licence and not true freedom. For his truth is in that which is universal in him. Individual human races also attain true freedom when they have the freedom of perfect revelation of Man and not that of their aggressive racial egoism. The idea of freedom which prevails in modern civilization is superficial and materialistic. Our revolution in India will be a true one when its forces are directed against this crude idea of liberty.

The sunlight of love has the freedom that ripens the wisdom of immortal life; but passion's fire can only forge fetters for ourselves. The Spiritual Man has been struggling for its emergence into perfection, and every true cry of freedom is for this emancipation. Erecting barricades of fierce separateness, in the name of national necessity, is offering hindrance to it. Therefore in the long run it is building a prison for the nation itself.

For the only path of deliverance for nations is in the ideal humanity.

Creation is an endless activity of God's freedom; it is an end in itself. Freedom is true when it is a revelation of truth. Man's freedom is for the revelation of the truth of Man, which is struggling to express itself. We have not yet fully realized it. But those people who have faith in its greatness, who acknowledge its sovereignty, and have the instinctive urging in the heart to break down obstructions, are paving the way for its coming.

India has ever nourished faith in the truth of the Spiritual Man, for whose realization she has made in the past innumerable experiments, sacrifices and penances, some verging on the grotesque and the abnormal. But the fact is she has never ceased in her attempt to find it, even though at the tremendous cost of losing material success. Therefore I feel that the true India is an idea, and not a mere geographical fact. I have come into touch with this idea in far-away places of Europe, and my loyalty was drawn to it in persons who belonged to countries different from mine. India will be victorious when this idea wins the victory—the idea of "Purusham mahantam adityavarnam tamasah parastat"—"The Infinite Personality, whose Light reveals itself through the obstruction of Darkness." Our fight is against this Darkness. Our object is the revealment of the Light of this Infinite Personality of Man. This is not to be achieved in single individuals, but in one grand harmony of all human races. The darkness of egoism which will have to be destroyed is the egoism of the Nation. The idea of India is against the intense consciousness of the separateness of one's own people from others, which inevitably leads to ceaseless conflicts. Therefore my own prayer is, let India stand for the co-operation of all peoples of the world.

The spirit of rejection finds its support in the consciousness of separateness; the spirit of acceptance finds its base in the consciousness of unity. India has ever declared that Unity is Truth, and separateness is *maya*. This unity is not a zero; it is that which comprehends all, and therefore can never be reached through the path of negation.

Our present struggle to alienate our heart and mind from the West is an attempt at spiritual suicide. If, in the spirit of national vainglory, we shout from our housetops that the West has produced nothing that has an infinite value for man, then we only create a serious cause of doubt about the worth of any product of the Eastern mind. For it is the mind of Man, in the East and West, which is ever approaching Truth in her different aspects from different angles of vision. If it can be true that the standpoint of the West has betrayed it into an utter misdirection, then we can never be sure of the standpoint of the East. Let us be rid of all false pride and rejoice at any lamp being lit in any corner of the world, knowing that it is a part of the common illumination of our house.

The other day I was invited to the house of a distinguished art-critic of America who is a great admirer of old Italian Art. I questioned him if he knew anything of our Indian pictures, and he brusquely said that most probably he would hate them. I suspected he had seen some of them and hated them already. In retaliation I could have said something in the same language about Western Art. But I am proud to say it was not possible for me to do so. For I always try to understand Western Art and never to hate it.

Whatever we understand and enjoy in human products instantly becomes ours, wherever they might have their origin. I am proud of my humanity, when I can acknowledge the poets and artists of other countries as my own.

Let me feel with unalloyed gladness that all the great glories of man are mine. Therefore it hurts me deeply when the cry of rejection rings loud against the West in my country with the clamour that Western education can only injure us.

It cannot be true. What has caused the mischief is the fact that for a long time we have been out of touch with our own culture and therefore Western culture has not found its true perspective in our life. Very often its perspective is wrong, giving our mental eye a squint. When we have intellectual capital of our own, the commerce of thought with the outer world becomes natural and fully profitable. But to say that such commerce is inherently wrong is to encourage the worst form of provincialism, productive of nothing but intellectual indigence.

The West has misunderstood the East. This is at the root of the disharmony that prevails between them. But will it mend matters if the East in her turn tries to misunderstand the West? The present age has been powerfully possessed by the West; it has only become possible because to her is given some great mission for man. We, from the East, have come to her to learn whatever she has to teach us; for by doing so we hasten the fulfilment of this age. We know that the East also has her lessons to give, and she has her own responsibility of not allowing her light to be extinguished. The time will come when the West will find leisure to realize that she has a home of hers in the East where her food is and her rest.

New York, *March 18th*, 1921

I wish that I could be released from this mission. For such missions are like a mist that envelops our soul —they seem to shut us off from the direct touch of God's world. And yet I have such an immense hunger for this touch. The springtime has come—the sky is overflowing with sunshine. I long to be one with the birds and trees and the green earth. The call comes to me from the air to sing, but, wretched creature that I am, I lecture —and by doing it I ostracize myself from this great world of songs to which I was born. Manu, the Indian lawgiver, enjoins us not to cross the sea. But I have done so; I have sailed away from my native universe—from the birthplace of those morning jasmines, from the lotus lake of Saraswati, which greeted me when I was a child even as the finger-touch of my own mother. Now, when occasionally I come back to them, I am made to feel that I have lost my caste; and though they call me by my name and speak to me, they keep themselves apart.

I know that my own river Padma, who has so often answered to my music with an amused gleam of tender tolerance in her face, will separate herself from me behind an invisible veil when I come to her. She will say to me in a sad voice: "Thou hast crossed the sea!"

The losing of Paradise is enacted over and over again by the children of Adam and Eve. We clothe our souls with messages and doctrines and lose the touch of the great life in the naked breast of Nature. This letter of mine, carrying the cry of a banished soul, will sound utterly strange to you in the present-day India.

We hold our mathematical classes in Santiniketan under the *madhavi*[1] bower. Is it not good for the students and others that, even in the busiest time of lessons, the branches overhead do not break out into a shower of geometrical propositions? Is it not good for the world that poets should forget all about the resolutions carried at monster meetings? Is it not right that God's own regiment of the useless should never be conscripted for any military contingency of the useful?

[1] White jasmine.

When the touch of spring is in the air, I suddenly wake up from my nightmare of giving "messages" and remember that I belong to the eternal band of good-for-nothings; I hasten to join in their vagabond chorus. But I hear the whisper round me: "This man has crossed the sea," and my voice is choked.

We are leaving Europe to-morrow and my days of exile are coming to an end. Very likely my letters will be fewer in number from now, but I shall make up for this when I meet you in person under the shadow of the rain-clouds of July.

Pearson is busy seeking health and happiness, making himself ready for the time when he will join us in India in the cold season.

S.S. "RHYNDAM"

The very fact that we have turned our face towards the East fills my heart with joy. For me my East is the poet's East, not that of a politician or scholar. It is the East of the magnanimous sky and exuberant sunlight, where once upon a time a boy found himself straying in the dim twilight of child-consciousness peopled with dreams. The child has grown, but never grown out of his childhood.

I realize it all the more strongly when some problem, political or otherwise, becomes clamorous and insistent, trying to exact its answer from me. I rouse myself, strain my mind, raise my voice for prophetic utterances, and try in every way to be worthy of the occasion, but in my heart of hearts I feel exceedingly small and, to my utter dismay, discover I am not a leader, not a teacher, and farthest of all away from being a prophet.

The fact becomes fully evident to me, that I had forgotten to grow. It comes of an incorrigible absent-mindedness. My mind has ever wandered away from those things that mature one into wisdom and old age.

I have neglected my lessons. And this utter want of training makes me such a wretchedly bad reader of journals dealing with the practical questions of the day! But I am afraid the present time is a tremendously difficult one in India for the child, the poet. It is no use protesting that he is lacking in understanding—that he is congenitally incapable of paying attention to anything urgent and serious. No, he must attend meetings or write editorials; cultivate cotton-fields, or accept some responsibility of grave and national importance, in order to make a fool of himself.

And yet my heart is aching and longing to meet, with proper ceremony, the first day of the rainy season, or fill every pore of my mind with the smell of mango blossoms. Is that allowable at the present moment? Does our south breeze still enjoy all the frivolities of spring days? Have our sunset hours taken the vow of discarding all traces of colours from their cloud turbans?

But what is the use of complaining? The poets are too primitive for this age. If they had not ignominiously been discarded by the law of evolution, they would long ago have grown into their career as politicians. But the mischief is--they have been left behind in a world which has stopped growing, where things are still important which have no use or market value. The more the call for action grows loud from across the sea, the more I feel conscious of something in me that cries: "I am of no use—leave me alone to my utter inutility."

But I know, when I reach India, the Poet will be defeated; and I shall piously study the newspapers—every paragraph of them. But for the present even poetry is at a disadvantage—for the sea is rough, my head is swimming, and the English language is extremely difficult to manage in a rolling ship.

S.S. "RHYNDAM"

Sometimes it amuses me to see the struggle for supremacy that is going on between the different persons within me. In the present condition of India, when the call is sure to come to me to take some part, in some manner or other, in some political affairs, the Poet at once feels nervous, thinking that his claims are likely to be ignored, simply because he is the most useless member in the confederacy of my personality. He fully anticipates that argument against him, and takes special pains to glorify his deficiency even before any complaint has been submitted by anybody on this point. He has proudly begun to assert: "I belong to the great brotherhood of the supremely useless. I am the cup-bearer of the Gods. I share the common privilege with all divinities to be misunderstood. My purpose is to reveal Purposelessness to the children of the Immortal. I have nothing to do with committee meetings or laying of foundation-stones for structures that stand against the passage of time and are sure to be trampled to dust. I am to ply the ferry-boat that keeps open the traffic between this shore and the shore of Paradise—this is our King's mail-boat for the communication of messages, and not for carrying cargo to the markets."

I say to him: "Yes, I fully agree with you; but, at the same time, take my warning, that your mail-boat may have to be commandeered for other urgent purposes, wholly unconnected with the Celestial Postal Department." His cheeks grow pale; his eyes become bemisted; his frail body shivers like a cypress at the first breath of winter, and he says to me: "Do I deserve to be treated like this? Have you lost all your love for me, that you can talk of putting me under martial law? Did you not drink your first cup of Amrita from my hand, and has not the Citizenship of the Sphere of Music been conferred upon you through my persuasion?"

I sit dumb, and muse and sigh, when sheaves of newspaper-cuttings are poured upon my table, and a leer is spread upon the face of the Practical man; he winks at the Patriotic man sitting solemnly by his side; and the man who is Good thinks it his painful duty to oppose the Poet, whom he is ready to treat with some indulgence within proper limits.

As for me who am the President of this *Panchayat*,[1] I have my deepest sentiment of tenderness for this Poet, possibly because he is so utterly good-for-nothing and always the first to be ignored in the time of emergency. The timid Poet avoiding the observation of the Practical and the Good comes to my side and whispers: "Sir, you are not a man made for the time of emergency—but for the time that transcends it on all sides."

The rascal knows well how to flatter, and generally wins his case with me—especially when others are too certain of the result of their appeal; and I jump up from my judgement-seat and, holding the Poet by the hand, dance a jig and sing: "I shall join you, Comrade, and be drunk and gloriously useless." Ah, my evil luck! I know why the chairmen of meetings hate me, newspaper editors revile me, and the virile call me effeminate! So I try to take shelter among the children, who have the gift of being glad with things and men that have no value.

S.S. "RHYNDAM"

My difficulty is that when, in my environment, some intense feeling of pride or resentment concentrates its red light within a certain limited area, I lose my true perspective of life and the world, and it hurts deeply

[1] Committee.

my nature. It is not true that I do not have any special love for my own country, but when it is in its normal state it does not obstruct outside reality; on the contrary, it offers a standpoint and helps me in my natural relationship with others. But when that standpoint itself becomes a barricade, then something in me asserts that my place is somewhere else.

I have not yet attained that spiritual altitude from which I can say, with perfect assurance, that such barricading is wrong, or even unnecessary; but some instinct in me says that there is a great deal of unreality in it, as there is in all passions that are generated through contraction of consciousness, through rejection of a great part of truth.

I remember your wondering why Christ gave no expression to His patriotism, which was so intense in the Jewish people. It was because the great truth of man, which He realized, through His love of God, would only be cramped and crushed within that enclosure. I have a great deal of the patriot and politician in me, and therefore I am frightened of them; and I have an inner struggle against submitting myself to their sway.

But I must not be misunderstood. There is such a thing as a moral standard of judgement. When India suffers from injustice, it is right that we should stand against it; and the responsibility is ours to right the wrong, not as Indians, but as human beings. There your position is higher than most of our countrymen's. You have accepted the cause of India for the sake of humanity. But I know that most of our people will accept your help as a matter of course and yet reject your lesson. You are fighting against that patriotism whereby the West has humiliated the East—the patriotism which is national egoism. This is a comparatively later growth in European history and a far greater cause of misery and injustice in the human world than the bloodthirsty ferocity, the nomadic savagery, in the primitive history of man. The Pathans came to India, and the Moghuls, and they perpetrated misdeeds in their heedlessness; but because they had no taint of patriotism they did not attack India at the very root of her life, keeping themselves superciliously aloof. Gradually they were growing one with us; and just as the Normans and Saxons combined into one people, our Muhammadan invaders would ultimately have lost their line of separateness and contributed to the richness and strength of Indian civilization.

We must remember that Hinduism is not the original Aryanism; in fact, a greater portion of it is non-Aryan. Another great mixture had been awaiting us, the mixture with the Muhammadans. I know that there were difficulties in its way. But the greatest of all difficulties was lacking—the idolatry of Geography. Just see what hideous crimes are being committed by British patriotism in Ireland! It is a python which refuses to disgorge this living creature which struggles to live its separate life. For patriotism is proud of its bulk, and in order to hold in a bond of unity the units that have their own distinct individualities it is ever ready to use means that are inhuman. Our own patriots would do just the same thing, if the occasion arose. When a minority of our population claimed its right of inter-caste marriage, the majority cruelly refused to allow it that freedom. It would not acknowledge a difference which was natural and real, but was willing to perpetrate a moral torture far more reprehensible than a physical one. Why? Because power lies in number and in extension. Power, whether in the patriotic or in any other form, is no lover of freedom. It talks of unity, but forgets that true unity is that of freedom. Uniformity is unity of bondage.

Suppose, in our Swaraj, the anti-Brahmin community

refuses to join hands with us; suppose, for the sake of its self-respect and self-expression, it tries to keep an absolute independence—patriotism will try to coerce it into an unholy union. For patriotism has its passion of power; and power builds its castle upon arithmetic. I love India, but my India is an Idea and not a geographical expression. Therefore I am *not* a patriot—I shall ever seek my compatriots all over the world. You are one of them, and I am sure there are many others.

S.S. "RHYNDAM"

Plato threatened to banish all poets from his Republic. Was it in pity or in anger, I wonder? Will our Indian Swaraj, when it comes to exist, pass a deportation order against all feckless creatures who are pursuers of phantoms and fashioners of dreams, who neither dig nor sow, bake nor boil, spin nor darn, neither move nor support resolutions?

I have often tried to imagine the banished hordes of poets establishing their own Republic in the near neighbourhood of that of Plato. Naturally, as an act of reprisal, His Excellency the Poet President is sure to banish from the Rhymers' Republic all philosophers and politicians. Just think of the endless possibilities arising from feuds and truces of these rival Republics—peace conferences, deputations of representatives, institutions with busy secretaries and permanent funds having for their object the bridging of the gulf between the two adversaries. Then think of a trivial accident, through which a hapless young man and a melancholy maiden, coming from the opposite territories, meet at the frontier, and owing to the influence of the conjunction of their respective planets fall in love with each other.

There is no harm in supposing that the young man is the son of the President of the Philosophers' Republic, while the maiden is the daughter of that of the Poets'. The immediate consequence is the secret smuggling of forbidden love-lyrics by the desperate youth into the very heart of the commentaries and controversies of the two contradictory schools of Philosophy—the one professed by the yellow-turbaned sages, proclaiming that *one* is truth and *two* is an illusion, and the other, which is the doctrine of the green-turbaned sages, asserting that *two* is truth and *one* is an illusion.

Then came the day of the great meeting, presided over by the Philosopher President, when the pandits of the two factions met to fight their dialectic duels finally to decide the truth. The din of debates grew into a tumultuous hubbub; the supporters of both parties threatened violence and the throne of truth was usurped by shouts. When these shouts were about to be transmuted into blows, there appeared in the arena the pair of lovers who, on the night of the full moon of April, were secretly wedded, though such intermarriage was against the law. When they stood in the open partition between the two parties, a sudden hush fell upon the assembly.

How this unexpected and yet ever-to-be-expected event, mixed with texts liberally quoted from the proscribed love-lyrics, ultimately helped to reconcile the hopeless contradiction in logic is a long story. It is well known to those who have had the privilege to pursue the subsequent verdict of the judges that both doctrines are held to be undoubtedly true: that *one* is in *two*, and therefore *two* must find itself in *one*. The acknowledgment of this principle helped to make the intermarriage valid, and since then the two Republics have successfully carried out their disarmament, having discovered for the first time that the gulf between them was imaginary.

Such a simple and happy ending of this drama has

caused widespread unemployment and consequent feeling of disgust among the vast number of secretaries and missionaries belonging to the institutions maintained, with the help of permanent funds, for the preaching of Union—those organizations which were so enormously perfect in their machinery that they could well afford to ignore the insignificant fact of their barrenness of result. A large number of these individuals gifted with an ineradicable passion for doing good are joining the opposite organizations, which have their permanent funds, in order to help them to prove and to preach that two is two and never the twain shall meet.

That the above story is a true one will, I am sure, be borne out by the testimony of even the august shade of Plato himself. This episode of the game of hide-and-seek of one in two should be sung by some poet; and therefore I request you to give it, with my blessing, to Satyendranath Datta,[1] that he may set it in those inimitable verse forms of which he is a master, and make it ring with the music of his happy laughter.

S.S. "RHYNDAM"

The sea has been exceedingly rough. The wild east wind, playing its snake-charmer's bagpipe, has made a myriad of hissing waves raise their hoods to the sky. The rude handling by the sea does not affect me much, but the gloom and unrest and the tremendous rise and fall of the waves, like a giant's beating of the breast in despair, depress my mind.

The sad thought very often comes to me, with an imaginary supposition, that I may never reach the Indian shore; and my heart aches with longing to see the arms

[1] A young poet of Bengal, greatly admired by Rabindranath Tagore. He has since, unfortunately, died.

of my motherland extended into the sea with the palm-leaves rustling in the air. It is the land where I gazed into the eyes of my first great sweetheart—my muse—who made me love the sunlight, touching the top of the coconut row through a pale mist of the serene autumn morning, and the storm-laden rain-clouds rolling up from some abyss behind the horizon, carrying in their dark folds a thrilling expectation of a mad outburst of showers.

But where is this sweetheart of mine, who was almost the only companion of my boyhood, and with whom I spent my idle days of youth exploring the mysteries of dreamland? She, my Queen, has died; and my world has shut against me the door of that inner apartment of beauty which gives the real taste of freedom. I feel like Shah-Jehan when his beloved Mumtaz was dead. Now I have left to me my own progeny—a magnificent plan of an International University. But it will be like Aurangzeb, who will keep me imprisoned and become my lord and master to the end of my days. Every day my fear and distrust against it are growing in strength. For it has been acquiring power from outside my own resources, and it is material power.

Santiniketan has been the playground of my own spirit. What I created on its soil was made of my own dream-stuff. Its materials are few; its regulations are elastic; its freedom has the inner restraint of beauty. But the International University will be stupendous in weight and rigid in construction; and if we try to move it, it will crack. It will grow up into a bully of a brother, and browbeat its sweet elder sister into a cowering state of subjection. Beware of organization, my friend! They say organization is necessary in order to give a thing its permanence, but it may be the permanence of a tomb-stone.

This letter of mine will seem to you pessimistic. The reason is I am unwell and utterly home-sick; and the vision of home which haunts my mind night and day is "Amader Santiniketan."[1] But the big towers of the International University obstruct its view. I am tired, to the marrow of my bones, trying all these months for a purpose and working in a direction which is against the natural current of my inner being.

S.S. "RHYNDAM"

You, who are given a stable and solid surface on which to work out your problems of daily life, cannot fully realize what a trial it has been for us, these two days, to be tossed upon a wild sea every moment of our existence. I do not feel sea-sick, but the great fact for us is, that we are the children of the land. This is an immovable fact—and yet, when this fact begins to move, it is not only misery, but also an affront to us. The whole sea seems to laugh loud at the conceited creatures who only have a pair of tottering legs and not even a fraction of a fin.

Every moment the dignity of man is outraged by making him helplessly tumble about in an infinite variety of awkwardness. He is compelled to take part in a very broad farce; and nothing can be more humiliating for him than to exhibit a comic appearance in his very sufferings. It is like making the audience roar with laughter by having the clown kicked into all manners of helpless absurdities. While sitting, walking, taking meals, we are constantly being hurled about into unexpected postures which are shamefully inconvenient.

When Gods try to become funny in their sublime manner of perpetrating jokes we mortal creatures find

[1] Referring to a song which the boys sing at the Asram, whose refrain is "Amader Santiniketan," meaning "Our Santiniketan."

ourselves at a terrible disadvantage; for their huge laughter, carried by the millions of roaring waves in flashing foam, keeps its divine dignity unimpaired, while we, on our side, find our self-respect knocked to pieces. I am the only individual in this steamer who is vying with the Gods by fashioning my misery into laughing words and refusing to be the mere passive instrument of an elemental foolery. A laughter which is tyranny has to be answered by another laughter of rebellion. And this letter of mine carries the laughter of defiance. I had no other object in sitting down to write this morning; I had nothing particular to say to you, and to try to think when the ship is rolling in such an insane manner is like trying to carry a full vessel of water while one is drunk; the greater part of the contents is spilt. And yet I must write this letter, merely to show that, though at the present moment I cannot stand erect on my legs, I can write. This is to assert, in the face of the ironical clapping of hands of the mighty Atlantic, that my mind not only can stand up straight in its world of language, but can run, and even dance. This is my triumph.

To-day is Tuesday; on the morning of Thursday we are expected to reach Plymouth. Your letters have helped me more than anything else during these extremely trying months of my exile—they have been like food and water to a soldier who is dragging his wounded and weary limbs, counting every step, across a difficult and doubtful road back to his camp-fire. However, I am coming to my journey's end and intensely hoping to see you when I reach home. What I have suffered God only knows.—I am longing for rest.

CHAPTER VIII

The few days spent in England on the Poet's return from America were on the whole happier and brighter than those of the previous year when the Dyer Debate in the House of Lords had poisoned the air. But he did not stay long enough to meet all those who were eagerly waiting his arrival. He had received invitations from every part of the Continent, and his time was short; for he had determined to get back to India at the earliest possible moment. In the letters from the Continent which follow in this chapter only a very slight portion of what actually happened is told. Many of his letters to me, at his own special request, have not been published; for in his self-diffidence he was almost ashamed, afterwards, to allow any record of the scenes of enthusiasm that greeted him everywhere to appear in print. Very rarely in history has a poet received such a welcome.

What touched him most deeply was the spiritual longing that was behind it all—the earnest hope, especially in the regions of Europe recently devastated by the war, that some light might come from the East to illumine the darkness. The ideal of Visva-bharati, which had become somewhat vague and nebulous before, now took on a more definite concrete shape. At the same time, he could not help but feel sadly that the cries of non-co-operation, which were so strident in India, would lead to his rejection by his own countrymen on his return.

Such a rejection did not take place, because in the heart of the national movement, under the leadership of Mahatma Gandhi, there was a common centre in the universal principle of Ahimsa, or Non-violence, which Mahatma Gandhi professed. No one admired more than the Poet Mahatma Gandhi's spiritual appeal against brute force and his passionate devotion to the service of the poor.

LONDON, *April 10th*, 1921

I am glad to be in England again. One of the first men whom I happened to meet here was H. W. Nevinson; I felt that man's soul was alive in this country, which had produced such a man as that!

A land should be judged by its best products, and I have no hesitation in saying that the best Englishmen are the best specimens of humanity in the world.

With all our grievances against the English nation, I cannot help loving your country, which has given me some of my dearest friends. I am intensely glad of this fact, for it is hateful to hate. Just as a general tries, for his tactics, to attract a whole army of men into a *cul-de-sac*, in order to demolish them, our feeling of anger generalizes the whole people of a country, in order mentally to give them a crushing blow on a tremendously big scale.

Things that are happening in Ireland are ugly. The political lies that are accompanying them are stupendous and in retaliation our anger seeks a victim adequately big; and we readily incriminate the whole people of

England, though we know that a great number of Englishmen feel shame and sorrow for these brutalities quite as keenly as any disinterested outsiders.

The fact that such a great proportion of people here—whose interest in keeping Ireland tied to the British Empire is so vital—can feel so keenly the tyranny inflicted on the Irish people, proves the inherent love of justice that thrives in the heart of this country in spite of all aberrations. The saving of a people depends upon the noble personalities holding up the moral tradition high above the floods of iniquity that occasionally deluge the land.

Edmund Burke proves the greatness of Great Britain in spite of Warren Hastings; and we are grateful to Mahatma Gandhi for giving India the opportunity to prove that her faith in the Divine Spirit in man is alive still—in spite of a great deal of materialism in our religions, as they are practised, and a spirit of exclusiveness in our social system.

The fact is that the best people in all countries find their affinity with one another. The fuel displays its differences, but the fire is one. When the fire comes before my vision in this country I recognize it as the same thing which lights our path in India and illuminates our house. Let us seek that fire and know that wherever the spirit of separation is supreme there reigns darkness. But with the realization of unity comes truth and light. When we ignite our lamps, we at once send response to the eternal lights of heaven. You yourself are a bearer of a lamp from your own land, and let me in response light my own lamp with love for the great humanity revealed in your country.

The following letter (a copy of which he enclosed) was in answer to a lady who had complained that the Poet had appeared to give vent to a feeling of anger against the British people in one of his lectures:—

LONDON, *April 12th*, 1921

DEAR MADAM,

I received your letter late that morning, and was sorry to learn that you had come to this hotel while I was engaged.

It is not unlikely that some unsuspected remnant of race-consciousness in your mind made you imagine that I gave vent to my feeling of anger against the British people in my lecture. I deeply feel for all the races who are being insulted and injured by the ruthless exploitation of the powerful nations belonging to the West or the East. I feel as much for the negroes, brutally lynched in America, often for economic reasons, and for the Koreans, who are the latest victims of Japanese imperialism, as for any wrongs done to the helpless multitude of my own country. I feel certain that Christ, were He living at the present day, would have been angry with the nations who attempt to thrive upon the life-blood of their victim races, just as He was angry with those who defiled God's temple with their unholy presence and profession. Surely He would have taken upon Himself the chastisement of these miscreants, especially when those who professed to be His disciples, whose ostensible vocation was to preach peace and brotherhood of man, either kept a discreet silence whenever man's history waited for a voice of judgement or showed signs of virulence against the weak and down-trodden greatly surpassing that of men whose profession it was blindly to kill human beings.

On the other hand, though I sometimes congratulate myself on my own freedom from race-consciousness, very likely a sufficient amount of it is lingering in my subconscious mind, making itself evident to outsiders in my writings through special emphasis of indignation at any unjust suffering or humiliation that my own country is made to undergo. I hope that I can claim forgiveness for this weakness, considering that I never try to condone any wrongs done by my own countrymen against others belonging to different countries from ours.

AUTOUR DU MONDE, PARIS, *April 18th*, 1921

I have come back to the domain of dust from my short aeroplane career in mid-air, when my namesake from the high heaven, the Sun[1] shed upon me his smile of amused tenderness and some vagabond clouds of the April sky seemed to wonder in their minds if I were about to join their ranks.

Whenever I find time and sit alone before the window, I gravely nod my head and say to myself in a sad voice: "Those who have been born foolish can gladden the heart of God only when they have the freedom of solitariness and can spread their idle wings in the air and flit and hum for nothing at all. You, poet, are one such creature—you have to be alone to fulfil your nature. What is all this that you are planning? Must you guide the multitude and work with them for the building of an Institution?"

All through my life I have ever worked alone; for my life and my work have been one. I am like the tree, which builds up its timber by its own living process; and therefore it needs leisure and space, sunlight and air and not bricks and mortar, masons and the civil engineer.

All my poems have their roots in my dreams. But an International University needs a foundation, and not

[1] Referring to his name Rabi, which means the Sun.

roots. It needs to be solidly built upon international boards and committees and funds contributed by men of prudence and foresight. Foresight is a gift which I wholly lack. I may have some insight, but no foresight at all. Foresight has the power of calculation: insight has the power of vision. He may have faith in insight to whom it belongs; and therefore he is not afraid of making mistakes or even of apparent failures. But foresight is impatient of all deficiencies. It constantly dwells on the possibilities of mistakes, only because it has not the vision of the whole. Therefore its plans are mostly solid and inflexible.

In the establishment of the International University the foresight of the experienced will never forsake me; it will go straight to the helm and take charge; and only then the prudent who give money and the wise who give advice will be satisfied. But where will remain the place for the foolish and the irresponsible?

The whole thing will have to be established on a permanent basis; but this so-called permanence is only bought at the cost of life and freedom. The cage is permanent, not the nest. And yet all that is truly permanent has to pass through an endless series of impermanences. The spring flowers are permanent, because they know how to die. The temple made of stone cannot make truce with death by accepting it. Proud of its bricks and mortar, it constantly opposes death, till it is defeated in the end.

Our Santiniketan depends for its permanence upon life. But an International University tries to build its permanence with the help of rules and regulations. But——

Never mind! Let me forget it for a moment. Possibly I am exaggerating. The reason is, the day is full of gloom. It has been snowing and raining; the road is muddy; and I am home-sick.

I am requested by some association to read a paper at one of their meetings. They asked me for a summary, which they will circulate among the members. I enclose a copy of it which I have given to them for circulation.

The Summary of a Lecture

From the beginning of their history the Western races have had to deal with Nature as their antagonist. This fact has emphasized in their minds the dualistic aspect of truth, the eternal conflict between good and evil. Thus it has kept up the spirit of fight in the heart of their civilization. They seek victory and cultivate power.

The environment in which the Aryan immigrants found themselves in India was that of the forest. The forest, unlike the desert or sea, is living; it gives shelter and nourishment to life. In such surroundings, the ancient forest-dwellers of India realized the spirit of harmony with the universe and emphasized in their minds the monistic aspect of Truth. They sought the realization of their souls through union with all.

The spirit of fight and the spirit of harmony both have their importance in the scheme of things. For making a musical instrument, the obduracy of materials has to be forced to yield to the purpose of the instrument-maker. But music itself is a revelation of beauty, it is not an outcome of fight; it springs from an inner realization of harmony. The musical instrument and the music both have their own importance for humanity.

The civilization that fights and conquers for Man, and the civilization that realizes for him the fundamental unity in the depth of existence, are complementary to each other. When they join hands, human nature finds its balance; and its pursuits, through rugged paths, attain their ultimate meaning in an ideal of perfection.

AUTOUR DU MONDE, PARIS, *April 21st*, 1921

When I sent my appeal for an International Institution to the Western people, I made use of the word "University" for the sake of convenience. But that word has not only an inner meaning, but also an outer association in the minds of those who use it; and that fact tortures my idea into its own rigid shape. It is unfortunate.

I should not allow my idea to be pinned to a word for a foreign museum, like a dead butterfly. It must be known, not by a definition, but by its own life-growth.

In the past I saved our Santiniketan School from being trampled into smoothness by the steam-roller of the Education Department. Our school is poor in resources and equipment, but it has the wealth of truth in it which no money can ever buy; and I am proud of the fact that it is not a machine-made article perfectly modelled in a workshop—it is our very own.

If we must have a University, it should spring from our own life and be maintained by our own life. Someone may say that such freedom is dangerous and that a machine will help to lessen our personal responsibility and make things easy for us. Yes! Life has its risks, and freedom has its responsibility; and yet they are preferable on account of their own immense value, and not for any other ulterior results.

So long, I have been able to retain my perfect independence and self-respect, because I had faith in my own resources and proudly worked within their sovereign limits. My bird must still retain its freedom of wings and not be tamed into a sumptuous nonentity by any controlling agency outside its own living organism. I know that the idea of an International University is complex, but I must make it simple in my own way. I shall be content if it attracts round it men who have neither name nor fame nor worldly means, but who have the mind and faith; who are to create a great future with their dreams.

Very likely I shall never be able to work with a Board of Trustees, influential and highly respectable—for I am a vagabond at heart. But the powerful people of the world, the lords of the earth, make it difficult for me to carry out my work. I know it, and I have had experience of it in connection with Santiniketan. But I am not afraid of failure. I am only afraid of being tempted away from truth, in pursuit of success. The temptation assaults me occasionally; but it comes from the outside atmosphere. My own abiding faith is in life and light and freedom. And my prayer is:—

"Lead me from the unreal to Truth."

This letter of mine is to let you know that I free myself from the bondage of help and go back to join with you the great "Brotherhood of the Tramps," who seem helpless, but are recruited by God for His own army.

STRASBOURG, *April 29th*, 1921

I am writing this from Strasbourg, where I am going to read my lecture at the University this evening.

I miss you very much at this moment; for I feel certain it would overwhelm you with happiness could you be with me now, realizing the great outburst of love for me in the continental countries of Europe which I have visited. I have never asked for it, or striven for it, and I never can believe that I have deserved it. However, if it be more than is due to me, I am in no way responsible for this mistake. For I could have remained perfectly happy in my obscurity to the end of my days, on the banks of the Ganges, with the wild-ducks as my only neighbours on the desolate sand islands.

"I have only sown my dreams in the air," for the greater part of my life, and I never turned back to see if they bore any harvest. But the harvest now surprises me, almost obstructs my path, and I cannot make up my mind to claim it for my own. All the same, it is a great good fortune to be accepted by one's fellow-beings from across the distance of geography, history and language; and through this fact we realize how truly One is the mind of Man, and what aberrations are the conflicts of hatred and the competitions of self-interest.

We are going to Switzerland to-morrow, and our next destination will be Germany. I am to spend my birthday this year in Zürich. I have had my second birth in the West, and there is rejoicing at the event. But by nature all men are *dwija* or twice-born—first they are born to their home, and then, for their fulfilment, they have to be born to the larger world. Do you not feel yourself that you have had your second birth among us? And with this second birth you have found your true place in the heart of humanity.

It is a beautiful town, this Strasbourg, and to-day the morning light is beautiful. The sunshine has mingled with my blood and tinged my thoughts with its gold, and I feel ready to sing:—

"Brothers, let us squander this morning with futile songs."

This is a delightful room where I am sitting now, with its windows looking over the fringe of the Black Forest. Our hostess is a charming lady, with a fascinating little baby, whose plump fingers love to explore the mystery of my eye-glasses.

We have a number of Indian students in this place, among whom is Lala Harkishen Lal's son, who asks me to send you his respectful regards. He is a fine young man, frank and cheerful, loved by his teachers.

We have missed this week's letters, which are now

evidently lost beyond recovery. It is difficult for me to forgive the Mediterranean for doing me this disservice! The present week's mail is due, and if Thos. Cook & Son are prompt about it we shall find our letters to-day!

GENEVA, *May 6th*, 1921

To-day is my birthday. But I do not feel it; for in reality it is a day which is not for me, but for those who love me. And away from you, this day is merely a date in the calendar. I wish I had a little time to myself to-day, but this has not been possible. The day has been crowded with visitors and the talk has been incessant, some part of which has unfortunately lapsed into politics, giving rise to a temperature in my mental atmosphere of which I always repent.

Political controversies occasionally overtake me like a sudden fit of ague, without giving sufficient notice; and then they leave me as suddenly, leaving behind a feeling of *malaise*. Politics are so wholly against my nature; and yet, belonging to an unfortunate country, born to an abnormal situation, we find it so difficult to avoid their outbursts. Now when I am alone I am wishing that I could still my mind in the depth of that infinite peace where all the wrongs of the world are slowly tuned up, out of their discordance, into the eternal rhythm of the flowers and stars.

But men are suffering all over the world, and my heart is sick. I wish I had the power to pierce this suffering with music and bring the message of abiding joy from the deeper regions of the world soul, and repeat to the people who are angry and to the people whose heads are bowed down in shame: "From joy all things are born, by joy they are maintained, and into joy they proceed and find their end."

Why should I be the one to air our grievances and give

shrieking expression to the feeling of resentment? I pray for the great tranquillity of truth, from which have welled forth the immortal words that are to heal the wounds of the world and soothe the throbbing heat of hatred into forbearance.

The East and the West have met—this great fact of history has so far produced only our pitiful politics, because it has not yet been turned into truth. Such a truthless fact is a burden for both parties. For the burden of gain is no less than the burden of loss—it is the burden of the enormity of corpulence. The fact of the meeting of the East and the West still remains concentrated on the surface—it is external. The result is, all our attention is diverted to this surface where we are hurt, or where we can only think of material profits.

But deep in the heart of this meeting is surely maturing the seed of a great future of union. When we realize it, our mind regains its detachment from the painful tension of the immediate present and attains its faith in the eternal—it is relieved from the hysterical convulsions of exasperated despair. We have learnt from our ancestors that the Advaitam is the eternal significance of all passing events—which is the principle of unity in the heart of dualism. The dualism of East and West contains that unity, and therefore it is sure to be fulfilled in union.

You have expressed that great truth in your life. In your love for India you carry that message of Eternity. In you, the apparent conflict of the East and the West has unveiled the great beauty of its inner reconciliation. We, who are clamouring for vengeance, only conscious of the separateness, and therefore expecting absolute separation, have not read the great purpose of our history right.

For passion is darkness. It exaggerates isolated facts and makes our minds stumble against them at every step.

Love is the light that reveals to us the perfection of unity and saves us from the constant oppression of the detached—of the immediate.

And therefore I embrace you, take my inspiration from your love and send you my birthday *namaskar*.[1]

NEAR ZÜRICH, *May 10th*, 1921

I have just received a birthday greeting from Germany through a committee consisting of men like Eucken, Harnack, Hauptmann and others, and with it a most generous gift, consisting of at least four hundred copies of valuable German books. It has deeply touched my heart, and I feel certain that it will find response in the hearts of my countrymen.

To-morrow I have my invitation at Zürich, and on the 13th of this month I leave Switzerland for Germany. Haven't I said to you, in some letter of mine, that my life has followed the course of my celestial namesake, the Sun, and that the last part of my hours is claimed by the West? How genuine has been the claim I never realized before I had visited the continent of Europe. I feel deeply thankful for this privilege, not only because it is sweet to realize appreciation from one's fellow-beings, but because it has helped me to feel how near we are to the people who in all appearances are so different from ourselves.

Such an opportunity has become rare to us in India because we have been segregated from the rest of the world. This has acted upon the minds of our people in two contrary ways. It has generated that provincialism of vision in us which either leads to an immoderate boastfulness, urging us to assert that India is unique in every way—absolutely different from other countries—or to a

[1] Greeting.

self-depreciation which has the sombre attitude of suicide. If we can come into real touch with the West through the disinterested medium of intellectual co-operation, we shall gain a true perspective of the human world, realize our own position in it, and have faith in the possibility of widening and deepening our connection with it. We ought to know that a perfect isolation of life and culture is not a thing of which any race can be proud. The dark stars are isolated, but stars that are luminous belong to the eternal chorus of lights.

Greece was not shut up in the solitude of her culture, nor was India, when she was in the full radiance of her glory. We have a Sanskrit expression, "That which is not given is lost." India, in order to find herself, must give herself. But this power of giving can only be perfected when it is accompanied by the power of receiving. That which cannot give, but can only reject, is dead. The cry, which has been raised to-day, of rejecting Western culture only means the paralysing of our own power to give anything to the West. For, in the human world, as I have said, giving is exchanging. It is not one-sided. Our education will attain its perfection, not by refusing to accept all lessons from the West, but by realizing its own inheritance. This will give us the means to pay for such lessons. Our true wealth, intellectual as well as material, lies not in the acquisition itself, but in our own independent means of acquisition.

So long as our intellectual attainments were solely dependent on an alien giver, we have been accepting and not acquiring. Therefore these attainments have mostly been barren of production, as I have discussed in my pamphlet on Education. But it would be wrong to blame the Western culture itself for such futility. The blame lies in our not using our own receptacle for this culture. Intellectual parasitism causes degeneracy in the intellectual organs of the mind. It is not the food, but the parasitism, that has to be avoided.

At the same time, I strongly protest against Mahatma Gandhi's depreciation of such great personalities of modern India as Ram Mohun Roy in his zeal for declaiming against our modern education.[1] Every Indian ought to be proud of the fact that, in spite of immense disadvantages, India still has been able to produce greatness of personality in her children, such as we find in Ram Mohun Roy. Mahatmaji has quoted the instances of Nanak, Kabir and other saints of mediæval India. They were great because in their life and teaching they made organic union of the Hindu and Muhammadan cultures—and such realization of the spiritual unity through all differences of appearance is truly Indian.

In the modern age, Ram Mohun Roy had that comprehensiveness of mind to be able to realize the fundamental unity of spirit in the Hindu, Muhammadan and Christian cultures. Therefore he represented India in the fullness of truth; and this truth is based, not upon rejection, but on perfect comprehension. Ram Mohun Roy could be perfectly natural in his acceptance of the West, only because his education had been perfectly Eastern—he had the full inheritance of the Indian wisdom. He was never a schoolboy of the West, and therefore he had the dignity to be a friend of the West. If he is not understood by modern India, this only shows that the pure light of her own truth has been obscured for the moment by the storm-clouds of passion.

HAMBURG, *May 17th*, 1921

It has been a perpetual sunshine of kindness for me all through my travels in this country. While it delights

[1] Mahatma Gandhi had been reported as saying that Ram Mohun Roy was a pigmy as compared with Kabir and Nanak, who had never had any touch with the West.

me, it makes me feel embarrassed. What have I to give to these people? What have they received from me? But the fact is, they are waiting for the daybreak after the orgies of the night, and they have their expectation of light from the East.

Do we feel in the soul of India that stir of the morning which is for all the world? Is the one string of her *ektara*[1] being tuned, which is to give the key-note to the music of a great future of Man—the note which will send a thrill of response from shore to shore? Love of God in the hearts of the mediæval saints of India—like Kabir and Nanak—came down in showers of human love, drowning the border-lines of separation between Hindus and Mussulmans.

They were giants, not dwarfs, because they had spiritual vision, whose full range was in the Eternal—crossing all the barriers of the moment. The human world in our day is much larger than in theirs; conflicts of national self-interest and race-traditions are stronger and more complex; the political dust-storms are blinding; the whirlwinds of race antipathy are fiercely persistent; the sufferings caused by them are world-wide and deep. The present age is waiting for a divine word, great and simple, which creates and heals. What has moved me profoundly is the fact that suffering Man in this continent has turned his face to the East.

It is not the man of politics, or the man of letters, but the simple man whose faith is living. Let us believe in his instinct; let his expectation guide us to our wealth. In spite of the immense distractions of our latter-day degeneracy, India still cherishes in her heart the immortal mantram of Peace, of Goodness, of Unity—

"Santam, Sivam, Advaitam."

[1] A one-stringed instrument.

The message of the "One in the All," which had been proclaimed in the shade of India's forest solitude, is waiting to bring reconciliation to the men who are fighting in the dark and have lost the recognition of their brotherhood.

Of all men in modern India, Ram Mohun Roy was the first man and the greatest who realized this truth. He held up high the pure light of the Upanishads that shows the path whereby the conquerors of the self "enter into the heart of the all"—the light which is not for rejection, but for comprehension.

The Mussulmans came to India with a culture which was aggressively antagonistic to her own. But in her saints the spirit of the Upanishads worked in order to attain the fundamental harmony between things that were apparently irreconcilable. In the time of Ram Mohun Roy the West had come to the East with a shock that caused panic in the heart of India. The natural cry was for exclusion. But this was the cry of fear, the cry of weakness, the cry of the dwarf. Through the great mind of Ram Mohun Roy the true spirit of India asserted itself and accepted the West, not by the rejection of the soul of India, but by the comprehension of the soul of the West.

The mantram which gives our spiritual vision its right of entrance into the soul of all things is the mantram of India, the mantram of Peace, of Goodness, of Unity—Santam, Sivam, Advaitam. The distracted mind of the West is knocking at the gate of India for this. And is it to be met there with a hoarse shout of exclusion?

HAMBURG, *May 20th*, 1921

I trust that my long voyage has now come nearly to its end. Every moment I hear the call of the beach and see the vision of the evening lamp watching behind the window for the return of the weary traveller. But there is one thought that never ceases to buzz in my mind. It is that the weather-beaten boat, after its voyage across the sea, may be utilized as the ferry for the miscellaneous errands of daily traffic.

To-day, life is nowhere normal in the world. The atmosphere is swarming with problems. Singers are not allowed to sing; they have to shout messages. But, my dear friend, is my life to be one perpetual polar summer, an endless monotony of a day of lidless light, of ceaseless duties, with never a night of stars to open before my vision the gateway of the Infinite? Is the fact of death a mere fact of stoppage? Does it not speak to us of our right of entrance into a region beyond the bounds of patriotism? When am I going to make my final adjustment of life and be ready for the invitation to the world of Spirit?

We are taught by our Western schoolmaster that there is nothing of importance that is not shown in the national school map; that only *my* country is my earth and heaven; that only in *my* country are united my life and my immortality. And when we try to reject the West, in our pride of country, we, like a ragged scamp, pick the pocket of the same West and pilfer that same spirit of rejection.

But our fathers had a clearer consciousness of a truth of freedom, which was never clipped of its wings and shut up in a geographical cage. I feel that my time has come for the realization of that truth; and I pray that I may never die a patriot, or a politician, but as a free spirit; not as a journalist, but as a poet.

STOCKHOLM, *May 27th*, 1921

I have been following the track of spring from Switzerland to Denmark, and from Denmark to Sweden, watching everywhere flowers breaking out in a frenzy of colours. And it seems to me like the earth's shouting of victory, and flinging up its coloured cap to the sky. My path in the West also has had the same exuberant outburst of welcome.

At first I felt the impulse to describe it to you in detail; for I was sure it would give you great delight. But now I shrink from doing it. For somehow it does not cause exultation in my own mind, but makes me sad. It would be absurd for me to claim what has been offered to me as fully mine. The fact is, there is a rising tide of heart in the West rushing towards the shores of the East, following some mysterious law of attraction. The unbounded pride of the European peoples has suddenly found a check, and their mind appears to be receding from the channel it had cut for itself.

The giant, being weary, is seeking peace; and as the fountain of peace has ever flowed from the East, the face of troubled Europe is instinctively turned to-day towards the East. Europe is like a child who has been hurt in the midst of her game. She is shunning the crowd and looking out for her mother. And has not the East been the mother of spiritual humanity, giving it life from its own life?

How pitiful it is that we, in India, are unaware of this claim for succour from Europe which has come to our door; that we fail to realize the great honour of the call to serve humanity in her hour of need!

Bewildered at heart by the great demonstrations made in my honour in these countries, I have often tried to find out the real cause. I have been told that it was because I loved humanity. I hope that this is true; and all through my writings, my love of man has found its utterance and touched human hearts across all barriers. If it *be* true, then let that truest note in my writings guide my own life henceforth!

The other day, when I was resting alone in my room

in the hotel at Hamburg, timidly there entered two shy and sweet German girls, with a bunch of roses for their offering to me. One of them, who spoke broken English, said to me: "I love India." I asked her: "Why do you love India?" She answered: "Because you love God."

The praise was too great for me to accept with any degree of complaisance. But I hope its meaning was in the expectation from me which it carried, and therefore was a blessing. Or possibly she meant that my country loved God, and therefore she loved India. That also was an expectation whose meaning we should try to appreciate and understand.

The nations love their own countries; and that national love has only given rise to hatred and suspicion of one another. The world is waiting for a country that loves God and not herself. Only that country will have the claim to be loved by men of all countries.

When we hear "Bande Mataram" from the housetops, we shout to our neighbours: "You are not our brothers." But that is not true. Therefore, because it is untrue, it pollutes the air, and darkens the sky. Whatever may be its use for the present, it is like the house being set on fire simply for roasting the pig! Love of self, whether national or individual, can have no other destination except suicide. Love of God is our only fulfilment; it has in it the ultimate solution of all problems and difficulties.

On the day after to-morrow we shall be leaving Sweden for Berlin. The Czecho-Slovakian Government has promised us an air trip from Berlin to Prague, and from Prague to Munich. From Munich we are expected to visit Darmstadt, where a gathering of some notable persons of Germany will be held to meet us. It will be over on or about the 15th of June, and then through France and Spain we shall be able to take our ship at the beginning of July—if not earlier.

BERLIN, *May 28th*, 1921

I am leaving Germany to-night for Vienna. From there I go to Czecho-Slovakia, and then to Paris—and then, to the Mediterranean Sea! Our steamer sails on the 2nd of July, and so this letter is likely to be my last.

You can have no idea what an outbreak of love has followed me and enveloped me everywhere I have been in Scandinavia and Germany. All the same, my longing is to go back to my own people. I have lived my life there, done my work there, given my love there, and I must not mind if the harvest of my life has not had its full payment there. The ripening of the harvest itself brings its ample reward for me. And therefore the call comes to me from the field where the sunlight is waiting for me; where the seasons, each in turn, are making their inquiries about my home-coming. They know me, who all my life have sowed there the seeds of my dreams. But the shadows of evening are deepening on my path, and I am tired. I do not want praise or blame from my countrymen. I want to take my rest under the stars.

BERLIN, *June 4th*, 1921

To-day my visit to Berlin has come to an end. To-night we are starting for Munich. It has been a wonderful experience in this country for me! Such fame as I have got I cannot take at all seriously. It is too readily given, and too immediately. It has not had the perspective of time. And this is why I feel frightened and tired at it—and even sad.

I am like a house-lamp, whose place is in a corner, and whose association is that of intimacy of love. But when my life is made to take part in a firework display, I apologize to the stars and feel humble.

I saw *Post Office* acted in a Berlin theatre. The girl who took the part of Amal was delightful in her acting, and altogether the whole thing was a success. But it was a different interpretation from that of ours in our own acting in Vichitra. I had been trying to define the difference in my mind, when Dr. Otto of Marburg University, who was among the audience, hit upon it. He said that the German interpretation was suggestive of a fairy-story, full of elusive beauty, whereas the inner significance of this play is spiritual.

I remember, at the time when I wrote it, my own feeling which inspired me to write it. Amal represents the man whose soul has received the call of the open road—he seeks freedom from the comfortable enclosure of habits sanctioned by the prudent and from walls of rigid opinion built for him by the respectable. But Madhab, the worldly-wise, considers his restlessness to be the sign of a fatal malady; and his adviser, the physician, the custodian of conventional platitudes—with his quotations from prescribed text-books full of maxims—gravely nods his head and says that freedom is unsafe and every care should be taken to keep the sick man within walls. And so the precaution is taken.

But there is the post office in front of his window, and Amal waits for the king's letter to come to him direct from the king, bringing to him the message of emancipation. At last the closed gate is opened by the king's own physician, and that which is "death" to the world of hoarded wealth and certified creeds brings him awakening in the world of spiritual freedom.

The only thing that accompanies him in his awakenment is the flower of love given to him by Sudha.

I know the value of this love, and therefore my petition to the Queen was:

"Let me be the gardener of thy flower garden"—the gardener, whose only reward is daily to offer his garlands to the Queen.

Do you think that *Post Office* has some meaning at this time for my country in this respect, that her freedom must come direct from the King's Messenger, and not from the British Parliament; and that when her soul awakes nothing will be able to keep her within walls? Has she received her letter yet from the King?

Ask Dinu what is the original of the following translation:—

My *Vina* breaks out in strange disquiet measure,
My heart to-day is tremulous with the heart-throbs of
the world.
Who is the restless youth that comes, his mantle
fluttering in the breeze?
The woodland resounds with the murmur of joy at
the dance lyric of the light,
The anklet-bells of the dancer quiver in the sky with
an unheard tinkle,
To whose cadence the forest leaves clap their hands.
The hope for the touch of a nearing footstep spreads
a whisper in the grass.
And the wind breaks its fetters, distraught with the
perfume of the Unknown.

To-day is the 5th of June. Our steamer sails on the 3rd of July.

DARMSTADT, *June 10th*, 1921

In Darmstadt they have a gathering of people from all parts of Germany to meet me. We have our meeting in the Grand Duke of Hesse's garden, where my audience will bring before me their questions. I give them monologues in answer, and Count Keyserling translates them into German for those who cannot follow my English.

Yesterday I reached this place, and in the afternoon we had our first meeting.

The first question put to me by a Canadian German was: "What is the future of this scientific civilization?"

After I had answered him, he again asked me: "How is the problem of over-population to be solved?"

After my answer, I was asked to give them some idea about the true character of Buddhism.

These three subjects took up fully three hours. It is delightful to feel the earnestness of these people. They have the habit of mind to think out the deeper problems of life; they deal seriously with ideas. In India, in our modern schools, we merely receive our ideas from text-books, for the purpose of passing examinations. Besides that, our modern schoolmasters are Englishmen; and they, of all the Western nations, are the least susceptible to ideas. They are good, honest and reliable, but they have a vigorous excess of animal spirits which seek for exercise in racing, fox-hunting, boxing-matches, etc., and they offer stubborn resistance to all contagion of ideas.

Therefore our English educationalists do not inspire our minds. We do not realize that ideas are necessary in order to enable us to live a true life. We do not possess a genuine enthusiasm, which is the gift of the soul. Our principal object and occupation are going to be the dissipations of politics, whose goal is success, whose path is the zigzag of compromise—that politics which in every country has lowered the standard of morality, has given rise to a perpetual contest of lies and deceptions, cruelties and hypocrisies, and has increased inordinately national habits of vulgar vainglory.

S.S. "MOREA," *July 5th*, 1921

Land has its claims upon one, in return for its hospitality, but sea has none; it repudiates humanity with a magnificent indifference; its water is solely occupied in an eternal dialogue with the sky—the two inseparable companions who retain their irresponsible infancy as on the first day of their creation.

Land imposes on us our mission of usefulness, and we have to be occupied with lectures and text-books; and our guardians have the right to rebuke us when we waste good paper in making literary paper-boats. But the sea has no inspiration of moral obligation for us; it offers no foundation for a settled life; its waves raise their signals and have only one word of command: "Pass on."

I have observed, on board a steamer, how men and women easily give way to their instinct of flirtation, because water has the power of washing away our sense of responsibility, and those who on land resemble the oak in their firmness behave like floating seaweed when on the sea. The sea makes us forget that men are creatures who have their innumerable roots and are answerable to their soil.

For the same reason, when I used to have my dwelling on the bosom of the great river Padma, I was nothing more than a lyrical poet. But since I have taken my shelter at Santiniketan I have developed all the symptoms of growing into a schoolmaster, and there is grave danger of my ending my career as a veritable prophet! Already everybody has begun asking me for "Messages"; and the day may come when I shall be afraid to disappoint them. For when prophets do appear unexpectedly to fulfil their mission, they are stoned to death; and when those whom men warmly expect to be prophets fail to act their part to the end, they are laughed to extinction. The former have their compensation; for they fulfil their purpose, even through their martyrdom. But for the latter, their tragic end is utter wastefulness; it satisfies neither man nor Gods.

Who is there to save a poet from disaster? Can anybody give me back my good-for-nothingness? Can anyone restore to me the provision with which I began life's journey to the realm of inutility? One day I shall have to fight my way out of my own reputation; for the call of my Padma river still comes to me through this huge and growing barrier. It says to me: "Poet, where are you?" And all my heart and soul try to seek out that poet. It has become difficult to find him. For the great multitude of men have heaped honours on him, and he cannot be extricated from under them. I must stop here—for the ship's engine is throbbing in a measure which is not that of my pen.

S.S. "MOREA," *July 6th*, 1921

I suppose you have read in the newspapers that in Europe I met with an enthusiastic welcome. No doubt I was thankful to the people for their kind feelings towards me; but somehow, deep in my heart I was bewildered and almost pained.

Any expression of feeling by a great multitude of men must have in it a large measure of unreality. It cannot help exaggerating itself simply because of the cumulative effect of emotion upon the crowd-mind. It is like a sound in a hall, which is echoed back from innumerable corners. An immense amount of it is only contagion—it is irrational, and every member of the crowd has the freedom to draw upon his own imagination for building up his opinion. Their idea of me cannot be the real me. I am sorry for it and for myself. It makes me feel a longing to take shelter in my former obscurity. It is hateful to have to live in a world made up of other people's illusions. I have seen people press round me to touch the hem of my robe, to kiss it in reverence—it saddens my heart. How am I to convince these people that I am of them and not above them, and that there are many among them who are worthy of reverence from me?

And yet I know for certain that there is not a single

individual in their midst who is a poet as I am. But reverence of this kind is not for a poet. The poet is for conducting ceremonial in the festival of life; and for his reward he is to have his open invitation to all feasts wherever he is appreciated. If he is successful, he is appointed to the perpetual comradeship of Man—not as a guide, but as a companion. But if, by some mad freak of fate, I am set upon an altar, I shall be deprived of my own true seat—which by right is mine and not another's.

It is far better for a poet to miss his reward in this life rather than to have a false reward, or to have his reward in an excessive measure. The man who constantly receives honour from admiring crowds has the grave danger of developing a habit of mental parasitism upon such honour. He consciously, or unconsciously, grows to have a kind of craving for it, and feels injured when his allowance is curtailed or withdrawn.

I become frightened of such a possibility in me, for it is vulgar. Unfortunately, when a person has some mission of doing some kind of public good, his popularity becomes the best asset for him. His own people most readily follow him, when other people have the same readiness—and this makes it a matter of temptation for such an individual. A large number of his followers will consider themselves as deceived by him when the fickle flow of popularity changes its course.

S.S. "MOREA," *July 7th,* 1921

In this modern age of the philosophy of relativity I suppose I cannot claim for myself the quality of absolute poetdom. It is evident that the poet in me changes its features and spontaneously assumes the character of the preacher with the change of its position. I have evolved in me a certain philosophy of life which has in it a strong emotional element, and therefore it can sing as well as speak. It is like a cloud that can break out in a shower of rain, or merely tinge itself in colours and offer decorations to the festival of the sky. For this reason I give rise to expectations which are almost of a contrary character—I am asked to give gladness, and I am asked to give help.

To give gladness requires inspiration; to give help requires organization—the one depends principally upon myself, and the other upon means and materials that are outside me. Here come in difficulties which make me pause. Poesy creates its own solitude for the poet. The consequent detachment of mind which is necessary for creative life is lost or broken when the poet has to choose a constructive programme. The work of construction requires continuous employment of attention and energy—it cannot afford to grant leave to the poet to retire and come to himself.

This creates conflict within my nature and very often makes me think that the guidance of the Good is not always for the Best. And yet, its call being natural to me, I cannot ignore it altogether. But what constantly hurts me is the fact that, in a work of organization, I have to deal with and make use of men who have more faith in the material part than in the creative ideal.

My work is not for the success of the work itself, but for the realization of the ideal. But those in whose minds the reality of the ideal is not clear, and love for the ideal is not strong, try to find their compensation in the success of the work; and they are therefore ready for all kinds of compromise.

I know that the idea which I have in mind requires the elimination of all passions that have their place in the narrow range of life; but most people believe that these passions are the steam-power which gives velocity to our motives. They quote precedents; they say that pure idea has never achieved any result. But when you say that the result is not greater than the idea itself, then they laugh at you!

During the last fourteen months of my campaign for an International University, I have said to myself over and over again: "Never let your pride be hurt at any prospect of failure; for failure can never affect truth. Strenuously keep all your attention on being true." My weakness creeps in where I love. When those whom I love feel exultant at the expectation of success, it urges me to procure this toy for them.

S.S. "MOREA," *July 8th*, 1921

I must not exaggerate. Let me admit that the realization of ideals has its external part, which depends for its development upon materials. And materials—both human and non-human—offer resistance to success, and therefore must not be lightly spoken of.

But what I had in my mind was this, that the mastery of grammar and the creation of literature may not coincide. Emphasis upon grammar may hinder perfectness of expression. Success in materials may go contrary to the fulfilment of ideals. For material success has its temptation. Often our idealism is exploited for the sake of obtaining success—we have seen that in the late war. In consequence, the battle has been won, but the ideal has not been reached.

Ever since the scheme of the International University has been made public, the conflict in my mind has been unceasing—the conflict between the vision of the ideal and the vision of success. The plan itself is big and has a scope for the ambition of men who love to show their power and gain it. It is not merely ambition which lures our minds; it is the wrong value which we set upon certain results. To be certain of the inner truth requires imagination and faith, and therefore it is always in danger of being missed, even when it is near at hand; whereas external success is obvious.

You remember how Chitra, in my play of that name, became jealous of the physical beauty lent to her by the Gods—because it was a mere success, not truth itself. Truth can afford to be ignored, but not to be allied to unreality for the sake of success.

Unfortunately facts are cited to show that all over the world the prudent and the wise are in the habit of making a pact with Mephistopheles to build roads to reach their God. Only they do not know that God has *not* been reached —and that success and God are not the same thing. When I think of all this, I feel a longing for the simplicity of poverty, which, like the covering of certain fruits, conceals and protects the richness and freshness of the deeper ideal. All the same, as I have said, the pursuit of success must not be abandoned for mere want of energy and spirit. Let it represent our sacrifice for the truth, and not for itself.

S.S. "MOREA," *July 9th*, 1921

All true ideals claim our best, and it cannot be said with regard to them that we can be content with the half, when the whole is threatened. Ideals are not like money. They are a living reality. Their wholeness is indivisible. A beggar woman may be satisfied with an eight-anna bit when sixteen annas are denied her; but a half-portion of her child she will never consent to accept!

I know that there is a call for me to work towards the true union of East and West. I have unconsciously been getting ready for this mission. When I wrote my *Sadhana* lectures, I was not aware that I had been fulfilling my destiny. All through my tour I was told that my *Sadhana* had been of real help to my Western readers. The accident which made me translate *Gitanjali* and the sudden and unaccountable longing which took me over to Europe at the beginning of my fiftieth year—all combined to push me forward to a path whose destination I did not clearly know when I first took it. This, my last tour in Europe, has made it definitely known to me.

But, as I have said before, the claims of all great ideals have to be fully paid. Not merely the negative moral injunction of non-violence will suffice. It is a truism to say that the creative force needed for true union in human society is love. Justice is only an accompaniment to it, like the beating of a tom-tom to the song. We in the East have long been suffering humiliation at the hands of the West. It is enormously difficult for us either to cultivate, or express, any love for Western races—especially as it may have the appearance of snobbishness or prudence. The talk and behaviour of the Moderate Party in India fail to inspire us because of this—because their moderation springs from the colourless principle of expediency. The bond of expediency between the powerful and the weak must have some element in it which is degrading. It brings to us gifts for which we can claim no credit whatever, except, perhaps, persistency of expectation and unbaffled employment of importunity.

Self-sacrifice on the part of the gainer, and not solely on the part of the giver, imparts true value to the gift. When our claims are feeble, and our method of realizing them is altogether unheroic, then the very boons granted to us make us poorer. That is why the Moderates in India look so pitifully obscure by the side of the Extremists.

However, my point is that, as an idealist, it is immensely difficult for me to nourish any feeling of love for those people who themselves are neither eager to offer it to us nor care to claim it from us. But never let me look at that condition as an absolute one. There are screens between us which have to be removed—possibly they are due to the too great inequality of circumstances and opportunities between the two parties. Let us, by every means in our power, struggle against our antipathies—all the while taking care to keep wide open channels of communication through which individuals, from both sides, may have facilities to meet in the spirit of good-fellowship. I cannot tell you how thankful I feel to you, who have made it easier for me to love your people. For your own relationship with India has not been based upon a sense of duty, but upon genuine love. It makes me feel sad when I see this lesson of your love being lost—when it fails to inspire our people with the realization that love of humanity is with you far truer than patriotism.

I deeply regret that you could not accompany me in my last tour in Europe, though I understand the reasons that prevented you. If you had been with me, you would have been able fully to realize the great truth of the mission we have undertaken. To the majority of my countrymen the course of experience through which I passed will ever remain vague; and my appeal to them to view the history of our own country in the large background of humanity is not likely to carry any force. For my work I shall ever depend upon your comradeship, and therefore I feel sad that the reality of the ideal which has possessed me has missed its one signal chance of coming close to your heart. The perspective against which you have been recently setting up your scheme of life has been vastly different from mine. You have taken up responsibilities that may have to follow their own channels away from those that I shall have to choose; and the loneliness of my task, which has been my fatality in my past life, will follow me to the end of my days. But I must not complain. I shall follow the call of my providence, and I know that to respond to it in my own manner is fulfilment in itself, whatever may be its results.

S.S. "MOREA," *July 12th*, 1921

For the last fourteen months my one thought was to bring India into touch with the living activities of the larger world of humanity. It was not because I thought that India would be the sole gainer by this contact, but because I was certain that when the dormant mind of India was roused from its torpor she would be able to offer something for the needs of the human race which would be valuable.

Through different modes of political co-operation and non-co-operation India has assumed up to the present an attitude of asking boons from others. I have been dreaming of some form of co-operation through which she would be in a position to offer her own gifts to the world. In the West the mind of man is in full activity. It is vigorously thinking and working towards the solution of all the problems of life. This fullness of intellectual vigour itself gives its inspiration to mental vitality. But in our Indian Universities we simply have the results of this energy, not the living velocity itself. So our mind is burdened and not quickened by our education. This has made me realize that we do not want schoolmasters from the West, but fellow-workers in the pursuit of truth.

My own aspiration for my country is that the mind of India should join its forces to the great movement of mind which is in the present-day world. Every success that we may attain in this effort will at once lead us directly to feel the unity of Man. Whether the League of Nations acknowledges this unity or not, it is the same to us. We have to realize it through our own creative mind.

The moment that we take part in the building up of civilization we are instantly released from our own self-seclusion—from our mental solitary cell. We have not yet gained full confidence that we have the power to join hands with the great builders—the great workers of the world. Either our boastfulness breaks its voice in unnatural shrieking or our self-denunciation makes an abnormal display of itself in an aggressive flutter of humility.

But I am certain that we have every claim to this confidence, and that we must do everything to realize it. We do not want bragging; we need for ourselves the dignity of the man who knows that he has some purpose to fulfil for all people and for all time. This has made me bold to invite students and scholars from different parts of the world to an Indian University to meet there our students and scholars in a spirit of collaboration. I wonder if this idea of mine will find any response in the hearts of my countrymen of the present day.

S.S. "MOREA," *July 13th*, 1921

In our music, each *ragini*[1] has its special scale in which some notes are absent and some are added, and the sequence of them is different in different *raginis*. The idea of India in my mind has its different *raginis*, presenting different aspects.

During my absence in the West my idea of India had its own special grouping of notes, and consequently the vision had its own special emotional value. When, in my travels, I was communicating with you, I had not the least notion that your India and mine were vastly different at that moment. I came to be aware of this fact when, at Aden, a number of Indian newspapers of different dates came into my hands. I felt, for the first time in these fourteen months, that I should have to make another attempt between my aspiration and my country.

But misgivings come to my mind as to whether any proper adjustment will be possible. I hate constant conflicts

[1] Mode or tune.

and bickerings—always to be shouting at the top of my voice in order to make myself heard above the shouts of other parties.

The India about which I had been dreaming belongs to the world. The India that I shall reach shortly belongs tremendously to itself. But which of these must I serve?

Months ago, while sitting each day at my window in a New York hotel, my heart had been aching morning after morning for the time of my return—the day that should bring me back to the arms of Mother India. But to-day my heart is sad—like this dark heaving sea, under the rainy sky. I have been wondering in my own mind, during the last few days, whether it was not my mission to remain in Europe at least another year, where I was asked to stay. But it is too late now. From this time forward I must make the effort to train my attitude of mind to a condition for which I am not ready.

S.S. "MOREA," *July 14th*, 1921

There is an idealism which is a form of egotism egregiously self-assertive. The confidence which one has in one's own ideas may not arise from an unmixed love of truth. It may be a subtle form of bigotry of self. There is an idealism ready to kill freedom in others in order to find freedom for its own plan.

I feel, at times, afraid lest such a tyranny of idealism should ever take possession of my own mind. For it would mean that my faith in truth had grown weaker than my faith in myself. Pride of self insidiously creeps into our schemes for ameliorating the conditions of our fellow human beings; and when failure occurs, we are hurt because the schemes are *our* schemes.

Egotism of this kind is blindly oblivious of other people's missions in life. It tries to impose one vast monotony of taste upon individuals who have temperament and capacities fit for other kinds of work. It is like the tyranny of conscription which compels teachers to dig and poets to kill their fellow-men. This, being against God's own purpose, is terribly wasteful. In fact, all tyrants in idealism try to usurp the rights of Providence for their own purpose.

The gloom of sadness which has been brooding over my mind for the last few days must be the shadow of my own egotism, whose flame of hope is dimmed by a fear. For some months I had been feeling sure that everybody would think my thoughts and carry on my work. But this confidence in me and in my plan has suddenly found a check and I am apprehensive.

No, this is wrong for me, and it is also a source of wrong for others. Let me be glad because a great idea, with all its beauty and truth, has alighted upon my mind. I alone am responsible for carrying out its commands. It has its own wings of freedom to bear it to its own goal; and its call is music, and not an injunction. There is no failure for truth—failure is only for me—and what does that matter?

Henceforth I shall have the chance of talking with you face to face. Yet distance has its own significance, and letters have their power of speech which tongues do not possess. And therefore, when we meet, some part of our thoughts will remain unuttered for the want of a great space and silence between us.

S.S. "MOREA," *July 15th*, 1921

Before I finish this last letter to you, my friend, let me thank you with all my heart for your unfailing generosity in sending me letters all through my absence from India. They have been to me like a constant supply of food and water to a caravan travelling through a desert.

I was sorely in need of them during the dreary months I spent in the United States. I promised to myself that I should try to pay you back in kind. I think I have kept my promise, and I hope you have got my letters in a regular weekly series, unless there have been gaps owing to the suspicions of professional eavesdroppers who watch over the destinies of the British Empire.

I suppose that the first few weeks I was lazy and depended upon Pearson to supply you with news, and therefore I am busy now in making up for the deficits. But about one thing I can never hope to compete with you. As a letter-writer you are incomparable! Mine are no more letters than lobsters are fish. They are like fragments of a book; like meteors that are shot off a planet. They are shot at you, and with a flash most of them vanish into ashes; whereas yours come down like showers of rain upon the thirsty land. Yet you must consider one thing in my favour—it is that I am heavily handicapped in my race with you, because I write in a language that is not my own, and this greatly adds to the original inertia I always have to overcome in writing any letter in any language whatsoever. On the other hand, writing letters is as easy to you as it is easy for our *Sal* avenue to put forth its leaves in the beginning of the spring months. However, I wonder if even *you* will be able to cope with my correspondence on my return! It has grown amazingly exuberant. Good-bye.

APPENDIX I

THE following letter was sent to the Editor of the *Manchester Guardian*, Mr. C. P. Scott, by Rabindranath Tagore, with reference to his friend W. W. Pearson, and was published on November 27, 1923:—

The news has reached us of W. W. Pearson's death through an accident which happened while he was travelling in Italy on the eve of his departure for India. He is not known to the wide public, but we feel sure that his loss is not merely a loss to the individuals who came into intimate touch with him. We seldom met with any-one whose love of humanity was so concretely real, whose ideal of service so assimilated to his personality, as it had been with him. The gift of friendliness, which he was ever ready to bestow upon the obscure, upon those who had nothing to attract the attention of their neigh-bours, was spontaneous in its generosity, completely free from all tinge of conscious or unconscious egotism, enjoying the luxury of the satisfied pride of goodness. The constant help which he rendered to those who were in need of it could have no reward in public recognition; it was as simple and silent as the daily fulfilling of his own personal requirements. His patriot-ism was for the world of man; he intimately suffered for all injustice or cruelty inflicted upon any people in any part of the earth, and in his chivalrous attempt to befriend them he bravely courted punishment from his own countrymen. He had accepted Santiniketan Asram for his home, where he felt he could realize his desire to serve the cause of humanity and express his love for

India, which was deeply genuine in his nature, all his aspirations of life centring in her.

I know he has numerous friends in this country and outside India who admire the noble unselfishness of heart which he possessed, and who mourn his loss. I feel sure they will appreciate our idea of setting up some permanent memorial in his name in our Asram, which was so dear to him. He had a great desire to see the hospital in connection with our institution rebuilt and equipped in an adequate manner, for which he was working and contributing money whenever possible. I believe if we can carry out this wish of his and construct a hospital building, and a special ward for children attached to it, this will be the best form of perpetuating his memory, reminding us of his sympathy for those who suffer.

APPENDIX II

THE following letter from the Poet to his friend W. W. Pearson was found among his papers and was too late for insertion in the last chapter of this volume. I have therefore included it as an appendix.

SANTINIKETAN, *July 4th*, 1923

I have just got your letter in which you ask me to give you my opinion concerning the importance of Institutional Religion.

As an abstract idea, I have nothing to say against it; for it is like the Caste System, perfect when ideally represented. Men can be classified according to their inherent differences in temperament. If all the natural Brahmins came together in order to carry on the special work which was only for them to perform, then through their mutual encouragement and co-operation an immensely potent force could be generated for the good of mankind. But directly a group is formed, its own group-personality almost invariably gives rise to an egoism which judges its own value by its external success and its physical duration. The Sect struggles for bigness and self-preservation even at the cost of truth. The growing consciousness of its own distinction and importance develops into a pride which—like the pride of wealth and office—becomes a temptation.

It is extremely difficult to become truly a Christian in conduct and life; but by following the easy path of belonging to a Christian Sect one seems to acquire the merit of being a Christian and also to have the right to despise even one's betters who by chance or by choice do not profess Christianity.

This has proved to be true of all religions which crystallize themselves into sectarianism. Religious communities are more often formed and established upon custom and the herd instinct than upon Truth. The children born to a Christian family are included in the religious community, not because they have shown in any way their fitness to belong to it, but because of the accident of birth. They do not have the time or the opportunity to discover their own individual inclination towards the religion they profess. They are persistently hypnotized into the belief that they are "Christians." For this reason we often witness the scene of men preaching Christianity as missionaries—or even as bishops—to their un-Christian fellow-beings, whom they might have killed as soldiers, or held down for ever under their heels as diplomats, had they followed their own true vocations.

An Institution which brings together individuals who are profoundly true and sincere in their common aspirations is a great help to all its members. But if, by its very constitution, it offers accommodation to those who merely have uniformity of habits and not unity of true faith, it necessarily becomes a breeding-place of hypocrisy and untruth. And because all organizations, by the very virtue of their power of combination, mechanically acquire a certain amount of force, such untruths and hypocrisies find ready opportunity to create widespread mischief.

Christ, like all other spiritual personalities, was solitary in moral greatness. He had a pure relationship of love and truth with all humanity. His Spirit works in solitude in the depth of men's souls. Therefore we find great-hearted individuals on the side of those peoples who are oppressed and insulted. On the other hand, we often find the Christian Church on the side of those vested interests which are engaged in exploiting the weak. This happens because the Church, as an organization, is a power which has its own natural alliance with other powers that are not only non-religious but very often irreligious. In fact, it is ready to make its bargain with those very powers that crucified Christ.

It is a truism to say that the character of the majority of the members constituting a religious community determines the level of its ideals. For this cause an Institution which is indiscriminate in the choice of its materials, and possesses an inordinate greed for the augmentation of its own numbers, very often becomes merely the most efficient organ for expressing the collective passion of its members. Have you not noticed this in the time of the late European War? And does not the profession of a sectarian Christianity fashion in the time of peace a cloak of respectability which covers a multitude of sins?

I know that a community of God-seekers is a great shelter for man. But directly this grows into an Institution it is apt to give ready access to the Devil by its back-door.

INDEX OF NAMES